Trust

KEY CONCEPTS IN THE SOCIAL SCIENCES

Published

Barbara Adam, *Time*
Alan Aldridge, *Consumption*
Alan Aldridge, *The Market*
Colin Barnes and Geoff Mercer, *Disability*
Darin Barney, *The Network Society*
Mildred Blaxter, *Health*
Harry Brighouse, *Justice*
Steve Bruce, *Fundamentalism*
Margaret Canovan, *The People*
Anthony Elliott, *Concepts of the Self*
Steve Fenton, *Ethnicity*
Michael Freeman, *Human Rights*
Russell Hardin, *Trust*
Fred Inglis, *Culture*
Jennifer Jackson Preece, *Minority Rights*
Paul Kelly, *Liberalism*
Anne Mette Kjær, *Governance*
Ruth Lister, *Poverty*
Michael Saward, *Democracy*
John Scott, *Power*
Anthony D. Smith, *Nationalism*

Trust

Russell Hardin

polity

First published in 2006 by Polity Press

Polity Press
65 Bridge Street
Cambridge CB2 1UR, UK

Polity Press
350 Main Street
Malden, MA 02148, USA

ISBN: 0-7456-2464-2
ISBN: 0-7456-2465-0 (pb)

A catalogue record for this book is available from the British Library.

Typeset in 10½ on 12 pt Sabon
by SNP Best-set Typesetter Ltd, Hong Kong
Printed and bound in Great Britain by T.J. International Ltd, Padstow, Cornwall.

For further information on Polity, visit our website: www.polity.co.uk

Contents

Acknowledgments   vii

1   An Age of Distrust?   1

2   Trust and its Relatives   16

3   Current Research on Trust   42

4   Social Capital and Trust   75

5   Trust on the Internet   98

6   Terrorism and Distrust   118

7   Liberal Distrust   135

8   Representative Democracy and Trust   157

Notes   180
References   185
Index   197

Acknowledgments

I thank the Kenneth Cole Foundation, Kenneth Cole, and Sam Marie Engle, Director of the Kenneth Cole Fellowship Program and of its Leadership Program at Emory University for sponsoring my lecture, An Age of Distrust?, as the Kenneth Cole lecture of January 2003. I thank many participants in that forum for their comments. I also thank Nomy Arpaly and Azi Lev-On for discussions of the internet and I thank Michael Baurmann for an extensive written commentary on part of this and for several recommendations to expand arguments. I also thank Mariel Ettinger, Andrea Pozas-Loyo, and Huan Wang for creative and energetic research assistance.

This book draws on the following prior publications. I thank the editors and publishers for being able to use and expand on some of their arguments here:

"Liberal Distrust," *European Review* 10, no. 1 (2002): 73–89.

"Terrorism and Group-Generalized Distrust," in Russell Hardin (ed.), *Distrust* (New York: Russell Sage Foundation, 2004), pp. 278–97.

"Internet Capital," *Analyse und Kritik* (Dec. 2004): 122–38.

For Robert J. Myers

Wonderful friend over many years (but
let us not count them)

1

An Age of Distrust?

Over the past decade or so trust has become a major worry of many scholars and pundits, very many of whom think trust is in decline in several of the advanced democracies, including Canada, Sweden, the United Kingdom, and the United States. To say that I trust you in some context is to say that I think you are or will be trustworthy toward me in that context. You might not be trustworthy toward others and you might not be trustworthy toward me in other contexts. If we think trust is declining, therefore, we must suppose that trustworthiness, or at least perceived trustworthiness, is declining. The value of trustworthiness is that it makes social cooperation easier and even possible, so that its decline would entail losses of cooperativeness. Most of the voluminous literature on declining trust sees it as a major problem independently of any account of trustworthiness – but surely if there is a problem here it is with trustworthiness.

This point is commonly ignored by many scholars, who see our problem as a failure of trust rather than of trustworthiness, and who argue for increasing trust – somehow. Of course, we do not simply want to increase trust per se, because we should not trust the untrustworthy. If we attempt to cooperate with you on some matter and you take advantage of our efforts, we should not readily risk cooperating with you again, and we should not trust you on the relevant matter. I want to discuss what it might mean that trustworthiness seems, at least superficially and also when examined more carefully, to be in decline. And I want to discuss what it suggests we should do to increase trustworthiness and cooperativeness – if we can or should do anything.

Declining trustworthiness would obviously be problematic at the personal level because it would increase the risks of attempting to cooperate with others. It might even lead us to avoid interactions with most others. It is less clear what follows from perceptions of declining trustworthiness among government officials. Presumably, if they are genuinely less trustworthy than they were four or five decades ago, we should suppose that government has deteriorated and, therefore, life has got worse for us. It is not easy to make a case for a general decline in prosperity, well-being, or many other desirable things that should supposedly correlate with declining governmental trustworthiness. There is a standard quip that things were a lot better back when things were worse. To claim that life in the advanced democracies has become worse for women, African-Americans, and those who are disabled in some way is simply perverse and malign. In the era of international terrorism and chauvinistic responses to it, life probably has become less pleasing to recent immigrants in the United States and perhaps in some nations of Europe. But huge numbers of individuals and several large groups have primarily benefited from the social and political developments of recent times even though levels of distrust in their nations may have risen during that period.

There are, of course, many uses of a term as attractive and seemingly good as trust. It would take us off track to do a deep conceptual analysis of various uses (see Hardin 2002b, ch. 3). But one small bit of linguistic history might be interesting. The word trust in English came into use in the medieval era. It developed with the word tryst in Middle English (Skeat [1879–82] 1910: 670; also see the *Oxford English Dictionary*). At that time tryst had a very simple meaning as a noun. Our village might mobilize to catch game – especially smaller game such as rabbits. Most of us would gather at one end of a wood or grassy meadow and would drive the game to the other end. At the other end, you might stand tryst, meaning you would be prepared to knock the rabbits in the head with a club. In that usage that's all the word meant. Tryst was a role. Forms of that word slowly took on two quite different meanings: the modern words tryst and trust. It's easy to see why linguistics might have gone those seemingly contrary ways. Standing tryst well meant to be trustworthy in the role one agreed to fill. And having a tryst with your neighbor's spouse behind the barn also entailed trust between you two misbehavers even while you violated the trust of your neighbor. So even in its linguistic origins, trust was a complicated affair. It still is. At least one person – your neighbor in the tryst – might not think trust is always so clearly a good thing. Trusting someone can set you up for cooperating with the other even in vile enterprises, as in the supposed honor among thieves.[1]

In the past century, if we'd been able to run surveys in the Soviet Union during the lifetime of Stalin, we would apparently have discovered astonishingly high levels of belief in Stalin's goodness bordering on religious faith. Perhaps no democratic leader has ever enjoyed very high levels of such belief – and certainly Gorbachev, Yeltsin, and Putin have not. Yet, most people who know the history of Stalin would not think he was trustworthy toward the Russian people and would think Gorbachev, Yeltsin, and Putin have been far more trustworthy than Stalin was. It took massive ignorance to believe in Stalin.

If trust or confidence in anyone can be so bad or so mis-guided, why do we typically think of it as a good thing? Largely because I am likely to trust you when you have given some evidence of being trustworthy. And if you are trust-worthy, I can cooperate with you to our mutual benefit. Of course, as in the case of those who thought Stalin was trust-worthy, I could be wrong in my assessment of you. But let us assume, what is probably true for most of us, that we are rea-sonably good at judging who is trustworthy or likely to be trustworthy in a particular standard context, especially after we have interacted with them for a while. Reference to a stan-dard context is important here because in standard, recurring contexts we will learn from experience, so that we will be better judges than we will be in novel and unfamiliar con-texts. Con artists take advantage of this simple fact by putting us into unfamiliar situations in which we supposedly would gain but in which we might far more likely lose.

Why Trust Now?

One may wonder: Why is trust suddenly an issue now? What has changed that makes us think distrust and untrustworthiness are on the rise? The political scientist Robert Putnam (2000) has written a large book on the topic of declining trust, although over the years in which he wrote he slowly changed his focus to speak of declining confidence, rather than trust, in government (Dalton, Pharr, and Putnam 2000). His book is mostly about what he characterizes as declining social capital. He says that the resources people, neighborhoods, and large communities once had to organize themselves to deal with problems have gone into steady decline in the US, beginning some time in the mid-1960s. (The notion of social capital is discussed more extensively in chapter 4.) During that period activities that isolate us from each other have steadily increased. For example, we watch television at home rather than playing cards at a neighbor's home. We drive our individual cars rather than taking public transportation. We live in scattered locations away from our places of work, so that our neighbors are not our fellow workers. We migrate far from our own families and friends. The community of Marcel Proust lived near enough to each other to call on each other to leave their cards on calling days. It is hard to imagine that practice today, although it was common in many communities a century ago.

Putnam's thesis is roughly that these two trends – rising distrust and declining social participation – are caused by the same things. The title of his book, *Bowling Alone*, is a metaphor for the general trend. We used to bowl in bowling leagues with others. Now we bowl more nearly alone without any particular organization of the activity. When Putnam first used the bowling metaphor, someone quipped that Timothy McVeigh and Terry Nichols had hatched their plan for blowing up the Alfred P. Murrah Federal Building in Oklahoma City while bowling together. Putnam could have answered, see, they developed the social capital that enabled them to do that awful thing. Of course, his general thesis is that social capital is typically a good thing, and he did not use such an argument.

The most precise and compelling of Putnam's reasons for the changes in social behavior is about the people he calls the "civic generation" – those people in the United States who came of age during the Great Depression and the Second World War. In the year Putnam's book was published, 2000, the youngest surviving members of that generation were about 76 years old – the oldest were about 92. That generation has stronger civic commitments than the generations that preceded them and than the generations that followed them. They are all too quickly passing from the scene.

When there is such a demographic pattern, we should consider two major possibilities. Either there have been demographic shifts in the overall population, or there has been a change in political circumstances. Because the American decline in overall civic mindedness begins in the 1960s, many people immediately think to explain the change as a result of Vietnam and the loss of credibility that the US government suffered then. Senator Trent Lott infamously might wish to explain it as the result of the end of legal segregation.[2] Some – including Putnam in part – have explained it at least partly as the rise of television to dominate our free time.

I wish to discuss two other changes that fit the pattern. One, discussed in chapter 8, is the increasing difficulty of formulating effective public policies to deal with complex issues such as poverty and crime. Lyndon Johnson's Great Society program arose and already showed signs of failure in the 1960s. The other is a pervasive change in the demographic conditions of our lives in comparison to those of earlier generations. Americans and Europeans typically lived in relatively homogeneous, often small communities in the early twentieth century and before. Few of them live in such communities today.

It Took a Village

Consider the recent demographic changes in the advanced democracies. There are two separate large demographic changes: the introduction of new groups in the advanced democratic societies; and changes in the way these societies live, with urbanization and suburbanization displacing small communities. Very few Americans or Europeans experience life in small communities today, although most Americans and Europeans came from such communities not long ago. Let us consider small communities and then turn to new groups in the society.

To begin, let's go back to life in a French village in the tenth century – over a thousand years ago. The Swedish economist Axel Leijonhufvud (1995; see further, Hardin 1999a) has described the life of Bodo, who lived in the parish of the church of St Germain, which kept substantial records of the lives of the parish. Today one would say that parish is in the center of Paris, but in Bodo's time it was a rural parish distant enough from Paris that many of its inhabitants may never have seen Paris. Virtually everything Bodo and his family consumed was produced by about 80 people, whom he presumably knew quite well. Moreover he knew them well over their entire lifetimes together. He probably knew almost all of them – those in his family and those not – better than we today know any but a very few people.

Most of what Bodo consumed was most likely produced by his own family. If anyone other than the 80 people of his small community touched anything he consumed, it was salt, which would have come from the ocean and would have passed through many hands on the way to St Germain.

Suppose we are in Bodo's village. There would be fewer than 80 of us alive at any one time. These would be all of the adults most of us would ever know or deal with. What a bore. Morality in such a society must be a compound of religious values and a form of quasi-reciprocity that is sometimes called social reciprocity or generalized reciprocity (Yamagishi and Cook 1993). When you have a serious problem, such as an illness or death in the family, the rest of us help out, each in our own way. I might bring you food or tend your garden or take care of your children. There may never be a time when you literally reciprocate by helping me. But whenever anyone else has a problem in our village, you reciprocate socially. We have to rely on each other to some extent and if I fail to be reliable everyone in the village will know and they may all sanction me, or even shun me. We have a communal norm of reciprocity (Cook and Hardin 2001).

This is a striking feature of Bodo's morality: that it is enforceable by the community. An enormous part of the debate about morality in the modern world – in philosophy, sociology, and psychology – is about how individuals can be motivated to act morally. That question is answered easily for Bodo's world. His community spontaneously enforced its morality as a set of compulsory norms. This did not guarantee perfect compliance, but it exacted a toll for noncompliance. Any of us who are utterly unreliable are likely to become pariahs to everyone else. At the extreme a cheater might have to leave the community and find another place to live. John Locke thinks that atheists cannot be moral and cannot be trusted to keep their promises because they don't face the threat of punishment in an afterlife. People in Bodo's village did not need that threat because they faced immediate sanctions in their lifetimes in this world.

Life for most people in Europe and the US two centuries ago was not so different from Bodo's. Peter Riesenberg (1992: 269) writes that

> in 1776 the overwhelming majority of Americans still lived in the kind of small-scaled community whose life and values . . . were essentially stable since the Greeks. In terms of law, social theory, and reality, and the relationship of secular and religious authority, Concord [Massachusetts], for example, resembled an English village of the late Middle Ages, or, indeed, ancient Sparta [in] the size of its population, its acceptance of community values and the community's regulation of public, economic, and personal life, in its constant search for the basis of harmony in the making of corporate decisions, its need for unity and homogeneity in religious affairs, its dependence upon shame to assure conformity, its intolerance of novelty and idiosyncrasy . . .

Life in these communities could be grim and oppressive (Wall 1990). As in Bodo's village, there was no need to worry about enforcement of morality as the townspeople saw it. They could humiliate and crush anyone who violated the local norms.

A Network Society

We are not in Bodo's village. As Leijonhufvud notes, the typical French citizen walking the streets of Bodo's St Germain today interacts indirectly with millions of people, not merely with 80. If you have a car, it includes parts from a dozen or more nations produced by perhaps thousands of people. We face relationships with vast numbers of other people, with whom we cannot expect to be in a rich enough network of broader relations to be able to ground enforcement of any norms. Relationships that can be organized by norms that are locally, spontaneously enforced are no longer part of many, if any, important aspects of our lives. We can't even expect that any norms we might hold dear would be shared by even the restricted set of all of those with whom we regularly deal. Our lives are radically different from Bodo's – not least in this respect.

In our more complex lives, we have many relationships that are about relatively specific things. Bodo's relationships were almost total. I know some people in one context and very different people in another context. I am part of many networks that are focused on some small range of matters and that have very little overlap in membership. In those networks, I become reliable at direct reciprocity. You do things for me and I return the favor. Or I might do something for you, you do something for Maria, and Maria does something for me. That may sound complicated but it is not that hard.

How do we regulate our relations in such networks? Basically, we develop trust relations with those with whom we deal reciprocally. I do something for you because I trust you to reciprocate. And you do reciprocate – in large part because you want to maintain your relationship *with me*. Because you want to maintain that relationship, you have an interest in fulfilling my trust in you; you *encapsulate* my interest in your own. (This is the encapsulated interest model of trust, which will be spelled out along with other models in chapter 2.) At least with respect to the matters covered by our network, we are trustworthy to each other. Anyone in our network who cheats anybody else in that network is likely soon to be excluded from the network. Because our network is a very small part of our lives, exclusion from it is not devastating, as exclusion from Bodo's community might have been.

Life in Bodo's village could be very nearly completely characterized without any mention of networks. All were connected to all on virtually every issue that went beyond family, and maybe even those external to Bodo's family tended to play roles within his family. Hence, there could be no specific network focused on a narrow matter from which Bodo could be excluded to sanction him for any minor infraction.

Peasant Life

Long after Bodo, but while agricultural production was still at the center of life for most people in the entire world, Marx ([1852] 1963: 123–4; cf. Hardin 1995: 39–42, 55) describes the peasants of France as so many homologous masses, like potatoes in a sack. In his account, it would be exaggerating to say that these peasants lived in communities. They were each involved with their own family members in subsistence farming for their own personal survival from day to day. They had little or no sustained interactions with others, because there was no return from cooperation or joint endeavors in their lives.

At the beginning of the industrial revolution, workers in factories were forced into cooperative endeavors daily, and they were given extensive opportunity to reflect collectively on the nature of their lives and, as Marx thinks, the extent of their exploitation by owners of their factories (Hardin 1995: 55). The workers therefore developed class consciousness, while the peasants, who did not daily and continuously discuss their common plight with each other, failed to understand their own interests. They therefore stupidly voted against their own interests in supporting Louis-Napoleon Bonaparte in the presidential election of 1848[3] (and in a plebiscite making him emperor, Napoleon III, at the constitutional end of his presidency in 1852). One can imagine that there is similarly restricted learning of interests in many other cases, more or less for Marx's reasons.

The condition of the peasantry as Marx describes it is not intermediate between Bodo and our society of networks because it was arguably less communal than Bodo's small society and it had almost no networks of economic significance. The peasant society is intermediate only in historical time. It is very nearly at the extreme of the possibilities for anomic organization – or disorganization – of life. The anomic disorganization of peasants may have been an important stage on the passage from virtual serfdom to independent individualism, but if so it was a grim transitional development. One might imagine that peasant society was deeply distrustful, because there was little possibility for mutually beneficial interactions, except within families. At its extreme, Edward Banfield (1958; see Hardin 2002b, 98–100) describes the moral basis of a backward society of subsistence farmers in his anonymously named Montegrano in the south of Italy in the 1950s. The farmers live in virtual isolation one family from all others. They share in no tasks and they never learn to cooperate on anything.

Terrorism and Ethnic Distrust

Unfortunately, there is a distressing part of Bodo's village story that still plays a role in our lives. If a stranger came from the outside into Bodo's village, the villagers would have been very wary and careful in their dealings with that person. The problem is not just unfamiliarity. It is that this new person is not embedded in the local norms and controls. Shunning the newcomer for any bad act would clearly not be an effective device because he can just leave – he is not tied to the village as the locals are. They are therefore at the newcomer's mercy to some extent, so they watch out.

The apparent hostility of small, close communities to outsiders might derive in large part from the fact that such communities cannot readily enforce their norms for behavior or their moral principles on outsiders who pass through. One might even expect a local community to hold outsiders not merely as strange but also as immoral. *The transition from such communities to larger, more diverse societies requires a transition in the basis of morality away from communally enforceable norms to ingrained, more or less abstract principles and to legal constraints.*

Apart from the nearly 3,000 lives lost and the increasing militarization of the US and the UK and much of the rest of the world, the worst ongoing effect of the terrorist actions of September 11 is perhaps the heightened distrust toward certain groups in the society – toward anyone who looks Arabic or South Asian. When we don't know someone, we often make an initial guess about them by fitting them to some stereotype. In some contexts stereotyping is wrong or illegal – for good reasons. But we do it all the time in ordinary contexts. If I see someone dressed like a woman, I'm likely to assume the person is a woman; I do that instantly without thinking it through. I might be wrong, especially where I live, in the Village in New York, but most of the time I will be right. Statistically, it's a good bet.

Now we face the possibility of a new version of discriminatory stereotyping that might be at least statistically justified. That is, the odds are that the most grievous terrorist attacks that Americans face will come from Arab and Islamist fanatics, although, as we know all too well, right-wing Caucasian Americans such as Timothy McVeigh are the next most likely source. In the United Kingdom, Spain, and some other democratic nations, the greatest threats may be domestic minority groups, not foreigners who import their terrorism. Part of the source of popular fear of Islamist fanatics is that they isolate themselves in exclusionary communities where we cannot know them and, perhaps more importantly, they cannot know us. They can sustain beliefs in such communities that would seem lunatic for anyone in the larger society, and their behavior might be governed by narrow communal norms. Their isolation coupled with suspicions about their actual beliefs and motivations may provoke a form of generalized or probabilistic distrust of everyone from their general background, the vast majority of whom are never going to be terrorists (see further, chapter 6). Note that what happens is individuals begin to distrust other individuals. In particular, non-Arabs are wary of people who look Arabic. People begin to think that Islam is a vicious and violent religion, although the blood shed by people in the name of Christianity must rival that shed by people in the name of other religions.

Concluding Remarks

Note that most of the changes mentioned earlier about why there has been a decline in civic mindedness are trends over which we have little control – generational change, television, demographic changes. So if these are the reasons for our supposed troubles, we are not likely to affect them. The one point on which we might be able to change things substantially is in our capacity to develop effective public policies for the hardest of our contemporary issues: education, race, terrorism, poverty, crime, drugs, immigration. A government that is competent enough to handle these well enough will seem trustworthy.

Even if we resolve these major policy issues, however, we are still in a world very different from that of our parents and grandparents. It is changed primarily, though not only, by technology, although technology has enabled us to leave the farm and go to cities, it has enabled us to make our own lives with less dependence on a particular local community, and it has also enabled us to craft our own individual lives in diverse ways, so diverse that we cannot expect government to be directly concerned with our welfare as, say, farmers once could.

Putnam and others, especially those who argue for deliberative democracy (for example, Gutmann and Thompson 2004, Skocpol 2003) or community (Etzioni 1993), descry our move from public to private involvement. They want us to restore the civic mindedness, the group activities, and the communal life that they think we have abandoned over the past 40 years. The economist Albert Hirschman (1982: 121) argues convincingly that moving from public to private involvements is very easy because any single individual can do it alone. Moving from private to public involvements is far harder, because we first have to mobilize a lot of people to construct the public sphere. Hirschman argues further that the shift from public to private was a liberating movement in the early days of the economic revolution that produced the wealth of recent centuries.

So are we in an age of distrust, and if so what does it mean for us? Yes, we are in an age of distrust if what that means is that we have more interactions with people whom we do not trust, and maybe even distrust, than we have with those we do trust. We do have more such interactions – but primarily because we have far, far more interactions of all kinds. We are not like Bodo – and we would not want to be. Many people say they prefer life in small towns and they dislike large cities. But far more people have chosen to live in large cities and, in the US, even more have chosen to live in the relatively large suburbs around large cities. Partly it is economic opportunity that drives people to cities. But for whatever reason, we overwhelmingly choose cities and their suburbs. Small towns are an anachronism in our lives and they should be treated as an anachronism in the work of social theorists, who should no longer argue that our lives are somehow wrong because they are not like those of people in small communities. We are the people who left those communities and we are not going back. The social theorists who praise small communities do so from academic pulpits at Harvard, George Washington, and other world-class universities. Along with most of the rest of us, they have left the communities that they praise. They are academic, not practicing communitarians.

We actively want to know more people than the 80 people Bodo knew. And we cannot imagine spending our entire lives within walking distance of the Paris of the Iles – even the Paris of a thousand years ago – and yet never going there. In our richer lives, we need trust relationships as Bodo did not. And we have trust relationships. In such relationships, we take risks on others, and when we take risks sometimes it doesn't go well and we wind up being cheated by someone and thereafter distrusting them and maybe similar others. To complain that rising distrust is bad, however, is to miss the point that if we are to have the possibility of interacting with – and trusting – more people, *we must have the other side of the coin: distrusting more people.*

The solution of our problem is not to try to return to or mimic the former world of very limited opportunities for both trust and distrust, but to learn how to live in our world. The world that is idealized by many social theorists was itself an unusual state of affairs. Two centuries ago, more than 80 percent of Americans and Europeans were farmers. Most of them were subsistence farmers. Their lives were hard and short and they did not generally live in communities like those that the social theorists like and praise.[4] The rise of small communities of moderately to very prosperous people was a strictly transitional phenomenon, and it cannot likely be recovered or recreated. All of this is a lot of change in our lives. The way to live with such change is to change ourselves or our behavior. In our world, we need networks of diverse people, not merely small communities – which all too often are exclusionary, closed communities. We create and live through manifold, relatively open networks and not through exclusionary groups and small communities.

Many of us would sooner live through such networks than in exclusionary groups. Of course, any one of our many networks is less rich than a community in various ways. But, taken together, these networks offer us much richer lives than a single community could do. In many ways our lives are far richer than those of our grandparents, and that greater richness has come from the evaporation of the kinds of community that many contemporary social theorists idealize.

An Overview of the Book

Chapter 2 lays out conceptual and theoretical issues in the nature of trust, especially in larger social and political contexts. It lays out the encapsulated interest conception of trust and relates that conception to the other two standard conceptions in the current literature. Chapter 3 takes up contemporary research on trust. That research has mostly been via experimental games and survey research. Game experiments primarily purport to address interpersonal trust issues. Surveys primarily address trust in government and trust in the general other person. The nature and role of social capital are taken up in chapter 4. Some of the debate on the supposedly rising levels of distrust in government and our fellow citizens has been framed (especially by Putnam 2000) as an issue in the decline of social capital.

Chapter 5 takes up the possibilities and difficulties of trust on the internet, which constitutes a new and remarkable form of social capital. The internet provides an extraordinary experiment in its own right in how well trust relations can be made to work in a relatively spare context that, however, has the basic element of standard trust theories: ongoing relationships. Chapter 6 addresses the way in which terrorism has provoked intergroup distrust, and the ways in which potential terrorists construct trusting relationships that enable them to hive off from the larger society and to co-operate in attacking it.

Chapter 7 addresses the nearly forgotten origins of liberal political theory, with its justification for distrust of government. We generally argue about distrust of government at the margin today, whereas the early proponents of liberalism were concerned with the core elements of a liberal society, which include fundamental distrust of government. Finally, chapter 8 addresses the current state of democratic theory and practice and the perhaps new turn back toward the position of liberal distrust in government.

2
Trust and its Relatives

Émile Durkheim rudely notes, "It has always been assumed that . . . in order to know the nature, role, and causes of the division of labor, it would be sufficient to analyze the notion each of us has about them" (Durkheim [1893] 1933: 46). Substitute "trust" for "division of labor," and we get a characterization of much of the literature on trust today and of virtually all of the vernacular and conceptually untheorized response to discussions of trust. Durkheim would disdain such a version of social scientific inquiry but would likely applaud the research focus on trust.

What we must want foremost is an explanatory account of trust, and in two senses. First, we must want a conception of trust that yields explanations of behavior and social institutions. Second, we must want a conception of trust that can be explained in its own right as the outcome of behaviors guided by some central concern or motivation of the relevant actors. One central concern is interests. Any account of such a major social category as trust must fit reasonably well with interests for at least some people, although surely not for all people.

In the current literature there are essentially three distinct conceptions of trust. All three are in fact conceptions of trustworthiness or, one could say, conceptions of how someone's trustworthiness of a particular kind leads us to trust that someone with respect to some matter or range of matters. As a rule, however, the literature would be much clearer and less confused if all proponents of all the extant theories recognized that their theories or conceptions are about trustworthiness and only derivatively about trust.

To say we trust you means we believe you have the right intentions toward us and that you are competent to do what we trust you to do. The three conceptions of trust vary in what would count as the right intentions toward the truster. One of these is the encapsulated interest account, which will be put to work in this book. It is grounded in an assumption that the potentially trusted person has an interest in maintaining a relationship with the truster, an interest that gives the potentially trusted person an incentive to be trustworthy (for early statements, see Schelling 1960: 134–5; Hardin 1982a: 186–7; for elaboration see Hardin 1991, 2002b). The other two conceptions ground the trustworthiness of the potentially trusted person in moral commitments or in the trusted's psychological or character disposition to be a relevant kind of person (one who keeps trusts). If trust turns on expected motivations of others, then trust is in a cognitive category with knowledge. All three of the extant standard conceptions are therefore cognitive because all depend on assessments of the trustworthiness of the potentially trusted person.

In the encapsulated interest conception, the right intentions on your part as a person we might trust are to want to take our interests (or possibly our welfare), as *our* interests, into account in your actions. You and we could have coincidental interests, so that, while acting in your own interests, you happen also to serve ours. If we know this and no more about your intentions, we can be confident of your actions, but we cannot be said to trust you. Distrust must have a similar logic. If we distrust you, that is because we think that your interests oppose our own and that you will not take our interests into account in your actions. In this view, trust and distrust are cognitive notions. They are in the family of terms that includes knowledge and belief.

If trust is cognitive, then we do not choose to trust. Rather, once we have relevant knowledge – of your moral commitments, your psychological or character disposition, or your encapsulation of our interests – that knowledge *constitutes* our degree of trust or distrust. To say we trust you means that we know or think we know relevant things about you, especially about your motivations toward us. Therefore one can mistakenly trust or distrust someone merely because one has wrong information about them. Many writers oddly suppose that trust itself – and not only acting on one's trust – is a matter of making a choice (see, for example, Bohnet and Zeckhauser 2004; Eckel and Wilson 2004; Sztompka 1999).

In the current wave of work on trust in government it is commonly assumed that trust can spill over from one agency or arena of government to others, so that your trusting local government can lead to your trusting higher level government. There is little or no evidence of such spillover; potentially definitive research on the issue has yet to be done. Gabriela Montinola (2004) argues, however, that there is spillover in a contrary sense: from distrust in one agency to distrust in another. Hence, here there may be an asymmetry, essentially an epistemological asymmetry, between trust and distrust. She argues that citizens typically cannot trust government because they cannot have the knowledge that it would take to define trust (see further, Hardin 2002b, ch. 7). But they can have enough knowledge to distrust specific institutions that are, for example, demonstrably corrupt. Montinola astutely notes that if higher level officials seem to take no action against openly corrupt officials, they give citizens reason to distrust government generally.[5]

Trust as Encapsulated Interests

The most natural and commonplace representation of the incentive structure of a trust relationship between individuals is as an exchange that cannot be consummated on the spot but in which the second party is required to fulfill after the first has done so or after the first has made a costly commitment whose benefit depends on eventual fulfillment by the second person. As a rule, we trust only those with whom we have a rich enough relationship to judge them trustworthy, and even then we trust only over certain ranges of actions.

Hence, trust is a three-part relation: A trusts B to do, or with respect to, X.

A full statement of the rational theory, including the incentive and knowledge effects, is roughly as follows. First, I trust someone if I have reason to believe it will be in that person's interest to be trustworthy in the relevant way at the relevant time. My trust turns, however, not directly on the Trusted's interests per se, but on whether my own interests are *encapsulated in the interests of the Trusted,* that is, on whether the Trusted counts my interests as partly his or her own interests *just because they are my interests* (in philosophers' jargon, the Trusted counts my interests as his or her own qua my interests). I may encapsulate your interests in my own, but this does not mean that your interests trump mine for me. Hence, there is some risk that my interests will trump yours and that I will therefore not fulfill your trust in me; and your trust will be limited to the degree to which you think my encapsulation of your interests gives them enough weight to trump other interests I have.

I might encapsulate your interests in my own for various reasons. Among the most important socially is that I wish to maintain my ongoing relationship with you. In this case, your interests have great weight for me because it is not merely the present fulfillment that matters but also all that might come from our long-run future interactions. I might also consider you my friend or I might love you and I might therefore actually take your interests as partly my own because I value you and your well-being sufficiently. Even if we do not directly have a relationship, I might encapsulate your interests to some extent in my own because I value my reputation in dealings with others. Because I encapsulate your interests in my own to some extent, I am likely to be trustworthy to some extent, and therefore you can trust me to that extent. A more general account simply includes a requirement that the trusted be trusted because, for some reason, she might be supposed to take the truster's interests into account in her choice whether to do what would fulfill the trust. Her reason might be moral concern or self interest, either directly or indirectly.

The encapsulated interest conception requires a mechanism by which I come to encapsulate your interests. In sum, there are three common mechanisms: we are in an ongoing relationship that I want to maintain because it is valuable to me; I love you or consider you my friend; or I value my general reputation, which could be harmed if I am untrustworthy in my dealings with you. The second of these mechanisms – the trusted's love or friendship for us – is in general unlikely to account for institutional-level trustworthiness. A recent American president may have said he felt our pain, but we could sensibly doubt that his feelings were very specific to us. The third of these mechanisms can apply in a large array of contexts, including those in which only my reputation with respect to some very well-defined matter is at issue, not my very general but strictly local reputation for cooperativeness in our small community. Even large corporations and other institutions can sensibly have a concern with their reputations for fair dealing and can therefore sometimes be seen as trustworthy (Dasgupta 1988).

Not included here are instances in which our interests happen to coincide, so that I do not take your interests into account but nevertheless do act in ways that further your interests. For example, when I drive on the right side of the road in North America, I am not acting out of the interests of other drivers – whom I do not even know and with whom I may have no other relationship other than that of once being near them on a highway – but out of my own direct interests in not being harmed in an accident. In such a case, we may be said to have coincident interests, but we do not encapsulate each other's interest.

A prisoner's dilemma or exchange model of trust

From this discussion, it follows that if our trust depends on ongoing relationships, so that we may say trust is a relational concept, it inheres in particular relationships. Moreover, it is likely grounded in the straightforward self-interest incentives of an iterated exchange relationship. As Hume says, "Constancy in friendships, attachments, and familiarities is commendable, and is requisite to support trust and good correspondence in society" (Hume [1751] 1975 (§4): 209).[6]

This view can be spelled out game theoretically, as will be done briefly here. Note, however, that one does not need to master the game theoretic model to understand trust relations in general. Although certain technical results may be hard to grasp without game theory, one can skip the discussion in this section without grievous loss.

Game theoretically, ordinary exchange can be represented as a prisoner's dilemma game (Hardin 1982b), as in game 2.1. In each cell of the matrix, the first payoff goes to the Row player and the second to the Column player, in the mnemonic Roman Catholic [R, C] convention. In this game, the outcomes show the payoffs to the players. For example, in the outcome (40, −30) the Row player's payoff is 40, while the column player's is −30.

Completing an exchange is equivalent to switching from the bottom right cell (0, 0) to the top left cell (15, 15) of the game. This move gives both players their second best payoffs, which are an improvement over their status quo payoffs that result from joint failure to cooperate with each other. If both players in a prisoner's dilemma cooperate, their outcomes are second best, with payoffs of 15 each. If one cooperates while the other defects, the cooperator does very badly (−30) while the defector does very well (40). If both defect, their payoffs are 0, as though they had not played the game at all, so that the outcome (0, 0) is the status quo ante. Play of the game can be iterated over and over, so that the possibility of affecting future possibilities affects choices in

		Column	
		Cooperate	Defect
	Cooperate	$15, $15	−$30, $40
Row			
	Defect	$40, −$30	$0, $0

Game 2.1 Prisoner's dilemma or exchange.

the present. Such iterated exchange does not define trust, but it is the context in which trust often arises.

Incidentally, the prisoner's dilemma game is by far the most studied of all games in game theory. That is largely because it models ordinary exchange, which is a pervasive form of interaction in our lives. Ironically, for many years it was studied primarily by psychologists, such as Anatol Rapoport, because of its seeming oddity. It was ignored by economists until fairly recently, although it represents the core element of economics: exchange. It is implicit recognition of its being the model of exchange that has led it to be the main focus of vast numbers of experiments on cooperation and now on trust.

In this model, trusting is typically a matter of self-interest but in a fairly specific strategic structure. Of course, that structure can be broader than a two-person prisoner's dilemma if reputational effects matter. If there were no reputational effects, we might often be able to play any given interaction as an endgame in which we would have no incentive to fulfill trust in us because there would then be no further interaction with that partner (this is Hobbes's implausible vision of the state of nature with only random encounters that are neither patterned nor repeated). Many ongoing interactions, in which the incentive is to be cooperative, might fail in the face of suddenly higher stakes, because then the incentive might be to treat the interaction over such stakes as a one-shot or endgame play (Hardin 1982a: 200–5). People who are seemingly honorable in living up to ordinary trust placed in them often turn out to be rascals in high stakes endgames. Hence, few of us, despite thinking we trust various friends, relatives, and associates, would risk lending them large sums of money without some contractual security to bind them to repayment.

Note that many theorists, perhaps most theorists, see trust as an issue in prisoner's dilemma or exchange interactions, especially with one player choosing first and the other choosing later. The broadly conceived iterated prisoner's dilemma account of trust is an encapsulated interest account. I trust you to be cooperative because I think it will likely be in your interest to cooperate when the time comes. But it will not merely be in your interest, it will be in your interest because of your concern for your relationship with me, broadly conceived to include reputational and other ramifications. That it would be in your interest to cooperate because the law would coerce you or because it would otherwise be in your interest independently of our relationship would be grounds for me to rely on you. But unless your interest in fulfillment encapsulates mine, my reliance on you is merely reliance and not trust. This account seems to fit most discussions of trust in broad social contexts and in the law. Vernacular use of the terminology of trust is much looser than this, but much of the vernacular usage is of little theoretical interest. For example, when a teenager says "Trust me" with a grin, the phrase is parasitic on the theoretically interesting notion of trust, not an instance of it.

If your trust of another is a bit or form of knowledge, then merely from inspection of the prisoner's dilemma matrix we can see that distrust and trust might be asymmetrical in an important sense. We can more easily come to distrust you than to trust you. The loss from your failing our trust is greater than the gain to us of your fulfilling it would have been. Consider game 2.1 with its payoffs in money. If Row defects while Column cooperates, Column loses $30. Column will then need two successful cooperations (at $15 each) to gain back that loss.

Note that, to make the prisoner's dilemma model trust relations, the game must be played more than once, or at least it must have the potential to be played repeatedly. It is the long-run payoff to each of us that makes the exchange inter-action desirable by giving each of us the incentive to be coop-erative. If we face a single prisoner's dilemma interaction, we have no such incentive and we might both defect, so that de facto we have no interaction (our payoffs are zero). More-over, note that once you distrust me – for example, if I defect in our first interaction – you may choose no longer to inter-act with me, so that you cannot gain the evidence that would be needed to show that you are mistaken in your judgment and that I am in fact capable of being trustworthy.

Reputation as an extension of encapsulated interests

Reputation is a centerpiece in many discussions of trust, but it is often characterized in a way that is misleading. For example, Sztompka (1999: 71) supposes that the value of your reputation is its value in my predicting how you will behave in certain contexts. He defines your reputation as simply the record of your past deeds. Hence, it becomes a predictor of your dispositions for certain kinds of action. Reputation does have these qualities, but its great importance in social life is *the incentive it gives the person who has a good reputation to behave in ways that sustain that reputation*. Reputational effects therefore extend the encapsulated interest model to indirect relationships. Your good reputation encourages others to choose you for various cooperative ventures that would be in your interest.

Firms pay heavily for reputations because they are valuable in this way. Individuals do likewise, although they do not typically spend resources on advertising. Once you have a good reputation, you are likely to want to maintain it and that fact gives me confidence to undertake dealings with you. The best way to establish a reputation is commonly not to tell others of your reliability but rather to demonstrate it very clearly in actual interactions. At the very large scale of our societies, we typically cannot expect many of those with whom we deal to know our reputations or to be able to rely on our incentives to maintain them.

This is a bigger issue than it might seem. Potentially cooperative relations outside our closer circles of relatives, friends, and frequent associates must often depend on confidence in others with whom we might never have occasion to interact again. Reputational effects can be very important in motivating such people to fulfill the cooperative ventures that we entrust to them. For many of us, such interactions are very common, so that the incentive effects of maintaining a reputation are very important to us. Often, of course, we resort to institutional safeguards, such as the law of contracts, to protect us in such contexts, but often there is no institutional safeguard that we can turn to. For example, if the scale of our exchange is not very large, the costs of resorting to a legally enforceable contract might outweigh the good that we seek in cooperating with each other. In large part because of the costs and difficulties of turning to institutions for ensuring our cooperative relationships, we find it sensible to protect our reputations by living up to them. Those with good reputations may tend to deal primarily with each other, so that the cost of not establishing or living up to one's reputation may be virtual exclusion from many kinds of cooperative venture.

Other Conceptions of Trust

In addition to the encapsulated interest view, as mentioned above there are two other conceptions of trust that are fairly widely invoked. One of these makes being trustworthy a matter of moral commitment. The other makes it a matter of character or disposition. The first of these is often framed as though the moral focus is on trusting rather than on being trustworthy. With few exceptions, however, almost all of the moral conceptions should properly be framed as about the morality of trustworthiness, and not about the morality of trust.

There are also many other idiosyncratic conceptions that are virtually unique to their first authors and that are seldom followed up by anyone else, other than to criticize them. Many of these must strike almost everyone but their authors as odd. In some accounts, trust is held to be founded in emotions or in virtually hard-wired dispositions (for a partial survey, see Hardin 2002b, ch. 3; for evolutionary accounts of such dispositions, see Kurzban 2003; de Waal 2003). Many of these accounts seem likely to fit some instances of trust or – perhaps more often – of trustworthiness. Little or no experimental work on trust addresses such accounts of trust, although a small fraction of the survey and interview work on trust arguably does. In general, these accounts have not been used to give us explanations of behaviors or of the structures of institutions. Hence, there is very little to criticize in them or to use from them, and I will not discuss them extensively here. Again, the focus in the present book is on explanation.

Arguments for many of the idiosyncratic views as well as many arguments for the three standard conceptions take the form of claims that "trust is" one thing or another. It is much more sensible to say that there are varied conceptions of trust. These conceptions are not theories, although because concepts are usually theory-laden we may expect different conceptions to lead to different theories of behavior and belief. The encapsulated interest conception leads to many explanations, as in this book (and in several chapters of Hardin 2002b and of Cook, Hardin, and Levi 2005).

The moral and dispositional conceptions have so far led to few if any explanations other than the definitional, virtually tautological explanation that those who are trustworthy out of moral or character commitments will be trustworthy. Then we face the task of identifying who these people are independently of their actions in the context we wish to explain, although for our close associates we can probably identify them successfully enough. Of course, we may be skeptical of the claim that someone is trustworthy tout court, no matter what incentives test their commitments, so even for these ostensibly extrarational conceptions of trust we may think they should be somewhat limited in the range of their applicability. That is, A will trust B but not with respect to every possible X. For trust as encapsulated interest, we can generalize the concern with interests to virtually everyone (except those who are psychologically odd or those who have exceedingly short time horizons). Hence, we can reach fairly general conclusions about people whom we do not even know very well. We may miss important details, but we will typically get the main story.

The three standard conceptions are sometimes called *strong* trust. What is evidently meant is that they are relatively restricted in their application. That leaves open the difficult question of what *weak* trust might be. It is without well-defined content. Indeed, in surveys it is essentially anything that any respondent thinks it is, so that it is simply the collection of the disparate vernacular notions of trust. Weak trust therefore must evidently entail weak theory, but we may hope that someone will take conceptual issues more seriously and will give us more articulate accounts of alternatives to the three standard conceptions.

Elements and Relatives of Trust and Trustworthiness

Trust is not a simple primitive term. It is constituted by certain things, including expectations and cognitive judgments of the motivations of others, motivations that would make them more or less trustworthy in particular contexts. And, if it is acted upon, it entails various things, such as risk-taking. Oddly, as noted in chapter 1, the focus of recent literature is on the need for trust rather than the benefits of trustworthiness, although trust could only make sense in dealings with those who are or who could be induced to be trustworthy. To trust the untrustworthy can be disastrous. If others are trustworthy, however, and we perceive this, so that we trust them, it can be in our interest to act on our trust of them, because that will enable us to have relationships that are mutually beneficial, relationships that might not be as readily regulated by standard legal devices, such as contracting under sanction of law. To say that trust would be good when others are trustworthy is not, however, to say that it would be good in general.

Reliance

All standard accounts of trust assume that it involves reliance on someone or some agency when there is at least some risk that the agent will fail the trust. To distinguish trust from mere reliance, as we rely on the sun's rising tomorrow, something more must be added to the notion. Some writers add morality (Hollis 1998). Presumably, moralized notions of trust are merely confused accounts of trustworthiness. Whether we should trust you, distrust you, or be neutral is typically a matter of prudential assessment, not moral choice. Indeed, in some contexts it would be not only imprudent but also immoral to trust someone. For example, it would have been immoral (and irrational) for an altruistic rescuer of Jews and others in Nazi Europe to trust random Nazi officials in their rescue efforts. If we entrust something to you, we are essentially relying on you and metaphorically making you our agent with respect to certain matters.

Risk

It is pointless to say you trust someone unless there is some risk of your suffering a loss if that someone does not fulfill your trust after you have acted on that trust to their initial benefit. The bulk of academic discussions of trust take this point for granted. If this point is correct, then you might trust one person with respect to a very large matter in which the loss from acting on the trust could even be catastrophic if the person did not fulfill. At the opposite extreme, you can trust another person with respect to very minor matters – such as reciprocation in buying coffee. You might not trust either of these people in the place of the other.

Much of the macrosociological work on trust by numerous scholars (including Beck 1992, Giddens 1990, Luhmann 1980, Seligman 1997, and sometimes Sztompka 1999) has associated the rise of concern with trust in modern societies with a supposed increase in the importance and intrusiveness of risk in our lives. Because these scholars do not give us compelling measures of risk in earlier times and today, it is very hard to judge what they mean and whether they are right. They cite such modern risks as the environmental disasters that we might bring on ourselves.

The thesis of increasing risk in our lives, even if we count only those risks that others (and not nature) impose on us, is implausible. Perhaps perceptions of risk have shifted, but that must be very difficult to show. In much of history, local communities were subject to the completely unannounced arrival of military hordes who descended upon them and summarily raped and murdered them and pillaged their lands. They were also subject to devastating diseases brought to them by visitors from other places. And they often precipitously destroyed their own environments (Diamond 2005), thereby destroying their entire civilizations and disappearing virtually without living residue. In part for these reasons, their lives were much shorter and radically poorer than are the lives of people in the advanced industrial states that are supposed to fit the thesis of trust as a response to harsh risk.

The supposition that things are much harder today is a variant of a golden age fallacy. It is an especially odd one in that it requires that things have got worse despite the apparent facts that in the advanced societies we are doing remarkably better today, that we live longer, healthier lives, and that our expectations are that we will continue to thrive. If there has been a golden age, it is more likely to be now than sometime in the past.

Expectations and confidence

In virtually all conceptions of trust, there is an element of expectations. Indeed, some accounts seemingly reduce trust to nothing more than expectations, as in such claims as "I trust that it will rain today," although the "it" that I trust has none of the features of a person whom I might trust (see, e.g., Barber 1983; Gambetta 1988: 217–18; Dasgupta 1988). Typically, accounts that go further and assume the rationality of trusting are actually accounts of the trustworthiness of others insofar as their trustworthiness is grounded in incentives of some kind that depend on the truster. Hence, we may say that rational accounts typically suppose that the truster assumes that the trusted will most likely prove to be trustworthy because it will be in the trusted's interest to act cooperatively with respect to the matters entrusted to her. Nevertheless, the trusted is not guaranteed to be trustworthy – she may have competing interests that trump – so that there is some risk in acting on trust.

When expectations are strongly positive, we may begin to speak of confidence. Much of the work on supposed trust in government might have little more to claim than that citizens are confident in their government (see chapters 3 and 8). Piotr Sztompka (1999) gives a lively account of the political and economic transition in Poland over the past couple of decades. He goes back to the mid-1970s to ground the sense of the roller-coaster ride that Poles have been on, with switches from good to bad days under the last decade or so of the Communist regime, and the even steeper roller-coaster ride they have experienced since 1989. In some ways, one might expect that respondents to the several surveys on confidence in government that Sztompka cites would have been even more volatile in their swings than they appear to have been, because the economic and political swings were in domestic affairs.

Sztompka does not give us the survey questionnaire items, so we cannot be sure just what Poles were claiming about their levels of trust. Even if we knew those items, however, we might still not be very confident of what it is we now know from the survey results. Clearly people seem to have more and less positive views of government and presumably many of them are willing to say that they trust the government. This fits Sztompka's view of trust as expectations of reliability. From similar survey studies in the United States and many other nations, it seems clear that we do not know very clearly what people mean when they answer particular questions that are then interpreted as trust items. The questions are notoriously poor but the responses to the few questions are nevertheless highly correlated. Perhaps it would already be good enough in the Polish case if all that the respondents are telling us is that they are confident that their government is now benign and maybe even competent. That might even be good enough in the case of other nations as well. But the Polish case is clearly an especially interesting and rich one.

As an aside, note that surveys can evoke prima facie implausible responses. Self-reported trust in President George W. Bush rose dramatically after the terrorist attacks of September 11, 2001. The administration had demonstrably failed badly and yet now people claimed to trust it more than before (*Economist*, June 8, 2002, pp. 27–8). It seems likely that the best way to read these weird results is to suppose that they are a patriotic move to rally round the flag, not an assessment of the trustworthiness of the regime.

Some accounts of trust do not specifically include reference to the trusted's interest in being trustworthy but merely require an expectation that the trusted will fulfill. Adequate reason for such an expectation, however, will typically turn on likely future incentives. Our actions in relying or not relying on you will also likely be tempered by past experience and reputational effects to a large extent, including your reputation for competence. If you never seem to understand the interest you have in future interactions, we will not take significant risks in trying to get you to cooperate. Those, such as many children, who are insufficiently future-oriented cannot be trusted. Those who are extremely present-oriented cannot generally act in their own future interest, even for the short term, and therefore they cannot be expected to act on the long-term interest they might have in maintaining a relationship for future benefits.

Note that the encapsulated interest account of trust is a rational expectations account in which the expectations depend on the *reasons* for believing that the trusted person will fulfill the trust. The typical reason is that the relationship is ongoing in some sense and that the trusted would like for it to continue. This is the unifying element for encapsulated interests: *the desire for the relationship to continue – for whatever reason, from merely financial interests, to deeper emotional ties, to reputational effects on other relationships.*

There are two especially important contexts for trust: ongoing or even strictly iterated two-person – or dyadic – relationships, and ongoing group or societal – or thick – relationships. The two classes are closely related and both are subsumed in the encapsulated interest theory of trust. These kinds of interaction – dyadic and group – pose incentives to the trusted. The sanction that motivates the trusted person in the dyadic trust interaction, if it is to be iterated, is the future benefits possible from the interaction, including gains (such as the pleasure of another's company) that are not themselves part of the direct gains in exchange. The implicit sanction that motivates both of the trusted parties in a mutual trust exchange interaction is withdrawal of the other party from a potentially beneficial interaction. And the sanction in thick relationships can be withdrawal from the dyadic interaction, as well as shunning from the whole community of those who share in the thick relationships, shunning that can be so severe as to exclude one from the community altogether (Cook and Hardin 2001).

Some Misconceptions

A commonplace argument in contemporary writing on trust is that we would all be better off if we were all more trusting, and therefore we should all trust more (Hollis 1998; Uslaner 2002). If we found a society in which distrust was endemic, we might readily conclude that its members would all or almost all be better off if we could somehow lead them to be more trusting by inducing them to be more trustworthy, perhaps by creating institutions that would substitute for trustworthiness while educating them to behave better. Yet we would plausibly recognize that it would not be in the interest of any individual in that society to simply start trusting (if that would even be possible conceptually[7]), because unstrategically acting as though one trusts can open oneself to exploitation. Similarly, Julian Rotter (1980) concludes that those who are more trusting are happier than those who are not, with the evident implication that to be trusting is per se good for us. But maybe those who are more trusting have good reason to be because they deal primarily with people who recognize the benefits of being trustworthy. It is not trust per se, but trusting the right people that makes for successful relationships and happiness.

Consider three worrisome issues common to the literature on trust. First, as already mentioned, most of the concern with trust is often better framed as a concern with trustworthiness. Throughout the growing literature on trust, there has long been and continues to be a tendency to say of trust what would be more applicable to trustworthiness. For example, Sztompka refers to a "trust culture" (1999: 99–101 and ch. 6). Some of the mystery in how we come to develop such a culture becomes less opaque if we focus on how we create trustworthiness in people and institutions. With respect to some things, particular individuals or institutions can establish their general trustworthiness even in the midst of generally untrustworthy others (again, it would be foolish to be generally trusting in such a context). If you come to see me as trustworthy in some context, then virtually by definition you have come to trust me. My trustworthiness might be a disposition grounded in moral commitments or character, but it might also be grounded in my recognition that being trusted by you and others will open me up to beneficial opportunities that would not be open to an evidently untrustworthy person.

Second, many discussions of trust could proceed just as clearly if the term "mere expectations" were substituted for "trust." Of course, without expectations of another, one would not be said to trust that other. We can be said to trust only if we expect fair reliability, and if we expect unreliability we distrust. But if there were nothing other than expectations at issue, the current trust literature would not exist.[8] It is expectations for the right reasons, such as the sense that the trusted encapsulates our interests to some extent.

Third, many writers either frequently or occasionally conflate trusting with acting on the trust. But there might be no occasion for me to act on my trust by entrusting some matter to you. Hence, my action and my knowledge of your trustworthiness – which constitutes my trust – are different. Sztompka (1999) speaks of "resorting to trust" (p. 14) and of "placing trust" (p. 25), and of trust as a resource (p. 16), a policy (p. 23), a strategy (p. 25), a commitment (p. 27), a decision (pp. 66, 69), and a kind of capital (p. 77). Many other writers similarly often treat trust as an action and therefore as a matter of choice (Bohnet and Zeckhauser 2004; James 2002; Eckel and Wilson 2004; Uslaner 2002).

Most of the writers who do this are making a mistake because they also treat trust sometimes as a matter of knowledge, which can give us reasons for action but which need not do so if no opportunity for relevant actions arises. For example, despite his moves toward making trust an action, Sztompka (1999: 97) also speaks of trust as a kind of knowledge with epistemological foundations. The latter view is the more compelling. Conflation of trust as a form of knowledge with trust as an action confuses analysis. Confusion of categories of such radically different kinds is unusual. Surprisingly, the passages in which Sztompka makes trust an action seldom actually matter for what he argues in his explanations of trust and the effects of trust, many of which are acute and almost all of which could as well be built on a conception of trust as a matter of knowledge. The frequent asides on trust as an action maybe mirror vernacular usage but play almost no theoretical role. Or they may be a tainted residue of the behavioral revolution and the insistence that we can only observe behavior, not thoughts or beliefs, which have to be inferred from actions.

Unfortunately however, the conflation enters many definitions of trust offered in the literature. For example, Sztompka's definition of trust is "commitment through action, or – metaphorically speaking – placing a bet" (1999: 26; also 69). Here Sztompka runs against vernacular usage, in which it is perfectly sensible to say I trust you even though I might not now have an occasion to act on my trust by entrusting something to you – I have no bets to place. Perhaps the most common way people use the term trust in ordinary life is simply to say that they trust some particular person, meaning that they would entrust certain matters to them but not that they do so in this moment or maybe ever. Sztompka's definition could be altered to speak of "potential action." Again, however, his definition of trust as "committing ourselves to action" makes little difference in his actual explanations of various social phenomena of trust. Indeed, it is not clear how the conception of "trust as commitment" could apply for most people when they say they trust the government. What action commitments do most of these people make?

Consider an example in which one supposedly chooses to trust. Sztompka (1999: 21) remarks that, in situations of helplessness in the face of, say, a terrorist's action or a president's decision on tax policy, "I simply have to resort to trust." (There are many similar claims throughout the literature.) On the contrary, I cannot "resort" to trust if I suppose that these two actors are at all likely to do what I do not want. I am merely helpless and, in the face of their likely untrustworthiness, I have no ground for trust, for belief in the benignity of these two powerful figures toward me. If I think the worst of them, I merely grit my teeth and try to survive their abuses. The only thing that can meaningfully force me to trust someone is evidence that they are likely to be trustworthy toward me in the relevant context, that they will have the right motivations.

The case of trusting one's president raises a different issue. Substantial power differences virtually wreck the possibility and meaningfulness of trust (Cook, Hardin, and Levi 2005, ch. 3). The more powerful agent need not trust the less powerful, who may have little choice but to do what the more powerful wants. And the less powerful cannot trust the more powerful because there is likely no reason to believe the more powerful party encapsulates the interest of the less powerful.[9]

Measurement of Trust

The most common way to measure trust, at least at the societal level, has been through surveys. Survey research findings on trust have been interpreted to suggest both that overall levels of interpersonal trust and that general levels of trust in government and other major social institutions are in steady decline in the United States, the United Kingdom, and some other industrial states. The popularization of the general conclusion of these studies has become a major part of public debates about the performance of government and the viability of democracy in an age of apparent distrust. These claims will be addressed in chapters 3 and 7.

Apart from directly asking people whether they trust, as in such surveys, almost all efforts to measure trust in some way involve game experiments. In such experiments the rationality of trusting or distrusting is sometimes de facto assumed. In standard game theory, the players are commonly assumed to be rational, although in experimental games, actual players often make quite diverse choices even when they face identical incentives. Therefore one might suppose either that the subjects make errors or that rationality is not determinately defined in interactive choice contexts. I think both conclusions are correct. Indeed there is no acceptable determinate theory that stipulates a best choice or a best set of choices of strategy in games in general (see further, Hardin 2003, ch. 2). Rather, there are many ostensible theories, none of them complete.

As a rule, levels of trust are taken to explain or predict levels of cooperation. Hence, trust is taken to be an important independent variable, although sometimes trust is itself the object of explanation. In much of the experimental literature, cooperation is taken to entail or be trust. Unfortunately, this means that trust is often identified with (or merely inferred from) cooperation and, because it is not independently measured, it yields no explanation of anything. Experiments that a decade ago were seen as tests of cooperativeness (often in plays of the prisoner's dilemma) are now more or less exactly repeated but are taken as tests of trust.

In conceptual work on trust it is commonly assumed that trust has two quite distinct dimensions: competence to perform what one is trusted to do, and motivation to perform. For example, I could distrust you to babysit for my child because I think you are incompetent, or because I think you would be malevolent to the child. Unfortunately, the main survey questions on trust in government (in the US National Election Studies series) do not separate these two dimensions. There are other data that suggest that citizens think the *integrity* of officials is not in decline and data that suggest they think the *competence* of officials is not in decline. The data on declining trust in government seemingly entail that citizens think that at least one of these is in decline.

The survey research asserting the decline of trust in the US and elsewhere is of too short a duration (a little more than four decades) to yield strong secular conclusions. The data on European nations other than Sweden and the United Kingdom are of much shorter duration still. There are other data, often much less focused, that tell us something about the longer term, but making sense of these is sufficiently difficult that it has spawned a large industry and many conflicting views.

Moreover, surveys measuring interpersonal trust gauge the extent to which people in general are judged to be trustworthy, whereas trusting behavior often depends on assessments of the trustworthiness of specific others. This raises questions about the limits of current survey evidence for enhancing our understanding of the behavioral manifestations of trust.

The two large demographic changes mentioned in chapter 1 might have changed the meaning of the responses to the standard trust questions over time. Increasing urbanization means interactions with larger numbers of people, so that "most people" is a much larger category for current generations than for similar people 40 or 50 years ago. Similarly, increasing immigration and increased mixing across ethnic groups suggest that "most people" is a more diverse category than it was earlier (see Alba and Nee 2003 on "remaking the American mainstream"). This effect might be part of the reason blacks are reported to be less trusting than are whites, because, as a mere structural fact, a black must have about seven or eight times more interactions with whites on average than a white has with blacks. The standard survey research questions addressing trust do not easily address these causal claims but largely mask them. Note however that younger people are less likely to say that most people can be trusted (Putnam 2000: 253). Their lives are more diversely urban than are the lives of previous generations. Their lives are also less settled and stable, so that they may have fewer of the relationships Hume cites as the foundation for trust (as quoted on p. 20 above).

These changes have been going on throughout human history. Among the things that technology and science have brought us are individual connections to vastly more people than anyone in earlier centuries could ever have had relations with. These vastly many people cannot be as well known to us as the villagers of, say, medieval times knew the several dozen people in their village, who, for many of those villagers, would have been almost the only people they would ever have met or dealt with. This change means that we must constantly size new people up as a normal part of our dealings. Sizing them up means judging their likely trustworthiness in dealings with us. Of course, there are risks in these dealings, but those risks are commonly small. The smaller they are, the less we need to worry about the trustworthiness of others. When the risks are very large, we want the backing of third parties and, especially, of institutions to enforce the cooperation we want. In an earlier time, we might have relied very heavily on our communal norms and their enforcement by all of us against any miscreant who behaved uncooperatively in certain contexts. But our lives have long since transcended such community.

It is these changes that are the most likely reason for our contemporary concern with trust and trustworthiness. Except during the dreadful era of mutual assured nuclear destruction, the risks that distinguish our condition are not risks of the catastrophic demise of all of us, or even many of us, but rather risks at the margin of opportunities that are more varied than what earlier generations have known. At the margin we face far more opportunities for cooperating for mutual benefit with a wider array of people (and organizations) over a wider range of issues than was true for our forebears. We therefore must face the risk of failed cooperation on more occasions and in more ways than did earlier generations. If we handle these interactions well, we benefit enormously. If we too conservatively avoid the risks of seizing on such opportunities, we lose enormously. The real change in risk-taking that has overcome us is those risks that we deliberately enter into individually, not those that roll over us collectively without our being able to contend with them. We virtually become the risks we are willing to take, for better or for worse.

Concluding Remarks

There are at least three standard elements that are often stated and two that are often entailed by or implicit in the rational accounts of trust. First, the relationship involves a Truster, a Trusted, and some matter that is at stake in the trust, so that it is a *three-part relation*. Second, the Trusted has some *incentive to be trustworthy* with respect to the matter at issue in the Truster's trust. Third, this incentive might be trumped by other considerations, so that there is some *risk* of default by the Trusted. Two other elements often implicit in these first three are that trust is *not a primitive term*, and that it is *cognitive*. To say it is not a primitive term means that it must be reducible to other terms, including the terms included in these standard elements. To say it is cognitive is to say that our trust in another is essentially a matter of relevant knowledge about that other, in particular knowledge of reasons the other has to be trustworthy.

Focus for a moment on the implications of the fact that trust is cognitive, that it is dependent on assessments of trustworthiness. It is commonly noted that familiarity and trust are linked. Why should this be? First consider the *benefits* of familiarity. Familiarity with another entails two things. Familiarity gives us *knowledge* about the other, in particular about the other's trustworthiness (of course, this means that it can give us the knowledge that another is untrustworthy). In addition, familiarity often derives from a relationship that gives the other person *incentives*. These are elements that make for trust, especially in the encapsulated interest model.

This suggests an epistemological assumption that people cannot know enough about their potential partners to trust anyone outside of very close – familiar – communities, which typically generate a lot of knowledge and incentives relevant to trusting someone. You may know your relatives, close friends, and a small number of coworkers and others you regularly deal with well enough to know the limits of their trustworthiness. Among these people you therefore know whom you can trust for what. Reputation can extend this group to a much larger group, but there are still severe cognitive limits on how many people one can genuinely trust.

Early work on trust, such as that by the psychologist Rotter (1967, 1971, 1980), focuses on individual-level trust. At this level, issues of trust and betrayal are rife in great literature, such as in two of Shakespeare's greatest plays, *Troilus and Cressida* and *Othello*, and in Tolstoy's great novels *War and Peace* and *Anna Karenina*. And they are central to our lives. Later work focuses on individual trust of institutions or institutional actors, such as professionals and other agents who are to act on behalf of individuals, who may or may not trust them (Barber 1983; Luhmann 1980). Very much of the recent work takes this concern virtually to its limit and focuses on individual trust in government (Warren 1999, Braithwaite and Levi 1998, Pharr and Putnam 2000, and many others). The most extraordinary claim in this last body of work is that the stability of government depends on the trust of citizens. This view is utterly contrary to the views of David Hume, James Madison, and many others who think that government should be distrusted. Their wary view is a foundational assumption of liberal political theory (see chapter 7).

Finally, some work along the way makes trust the basis of fairly grand social theory. For example, some of this work discusses the effects of trust on the atmosphere of cooperativeness in the larger society (Arrow 1974; Putnam 1993; Fukuyama 1995). Martin Hollis (1998: 23) speculates that trust and economic progress have a perverse, perhaps circular interaction. The more we trust each other, the better we are able to cooperate and therefore the better are our prospects for economic progress. He goes on to conclude negatively that with greater economic success we become more instrumentally rational and therefore we trust less.[10] Although many arguments in this work sound plausible, virtually none of this last body of work makes claims that could be tested in some evident way.

It is a striking fact that the Madisonian view on distrust of government prevailed in American political thought for well over a century. Today, however, that view is mostly espoused by conservatives and left-libertarians, while among liberals it has largely been displaced by the view that citizen trust in government is good and even necessary. This change in view would have to depend on the belief that government has actually become more trustworthy than it was in the time of the rule of King George III and the early American government. Something like the Madisonian view has also been prevalent in English thought for many centuries, as argued by such British thinkers as David Hume, Adam Smith, H. B. Acton, and Michael Oakeshott. However, with the possible exception of Margaret Thatcher's Tory party, no major party has campaigned on a platform of such a view, and the alternative view, that citizens should trust their government, is perhaps more widespread.

The best way to address these issues is to begin at the individual level and then to proceed to the societal and governmental levels. It is much easier to be clear about what is meant by the terms trust, distrust, and trustworthiness in individuals' relations with each other than in the larger societal and governmental contexts. Analytically, the strongest body of work on trust is about dyadic relational trust, that is, trust that is grounded in an ongoing relationship. This is the context in which use of the term trust presumably first arises historically. The largest body of data may well be that which purports to assess trust in government. One of the things that becomes clear once the individual-level problem is understood is that trust in government cannot mean the same thing as trust in a friend or relative or other person. Trust in government is cognitively far too demanding to be a credible issue. Yet, contemporary discussions of declining trust in government often seem to suggest that all of the moral censure that we might apply to failures of trust and trust-worthiness between close friends come to bear on the relations between citizens and their government.

3
Current Research on Trust

As noted, recent research on trust has been based primarily on game experiments and surveys. The experimental literature is mostly about individual-level trust in other individuals, usually in dyadic interactions. More accurately, we can say this research typically tests subjects' tendency to cooperate with each other, and trust is inferred from cooperative moves in games. Survey work has mostly been about citizens' stance toward government and other agencies, although some of it also addresses individual trust in others, often in the supposed general other (under the label generalized or social trust). The earliest research that was rigorous was on the psychology of trusting, as in the work of Julian Rotter (1967, 1971, 1980).

It is a peculiar fact that most of the current research, both gaming and survey, does not use clear accounts of what is being measured. Neither did Rotter, although he developed a trust scale for measuring trust, whatever trust might be.[11] In most of this academic research, trust is a term that is as loosely used as it is in the vernacular, where its meanings are many, varied, and often opaque. Trust is therefore treated as an a-theoretical term. It is, for example, all of the things that survey respondents think it is.

Neither of these two large bodies of empirical research on trust is very compelling. Surprisingly often, the point of such research is to go no further than to show that people ostensibly do trust. The experiments – especially those based on one-shot plays of variants of the so-called trust game – are often far removed from anything we would normally call trust in ordinary life and cannot be related to any of the standard conceptions of trust. To call the standard game in this literature the trust game is a bit of persuasive definition. I will call it and its variants the T-game. The surveys suffer the problem of many surveys that they are far too vague to yield clear conclusions. The principal survey questions were designed for other purposes and are simply applied, usually without any adaptation of the content of the questions, to the later concern with trust. It is therefore not surprising that they do not articulately address differences in particular conceptions of trust. Here I will first discuss the experimental gaming work and then the survey work.

Experiments on Trust

There is a long-standing, substantial body of experimental game research on problems of cooperation under several labels, including prisoner's dilemma, collective action, and social dilemma. The forms of the games in various experiments vary enormously, but most of them are prisoner's dilemmas (as discussed in chapter 2, and as represented in game 3.1 below), ranging from two to many persons. Or they are variants of the T-game (as in games 3.2–4). Work focuses on isolated interactions as well as on social contexts in which cooperative (or uncooperative) play evolves over many interactions. Many of the researchers doing experimental work have recently shifted their focus from explaining cooperation to modeling and measuring trust (see further, Cook and Cooper 2003). Although it would be wrong to say that if there is cooperation, then there must have been trust, it is commonly assumed in much of this work that successful cooperation indicates some degree of trust among the players. Recent efforts to introduce extra elements into the games might serve to test not merely for cooperation but for trust.

Column

	Cooperate	Not cooperate
Cooperate	15, 15	–30, 40
Row		
Not Cooperate	40, –30	0, 0

Game 3.1   Prisoner's dilemma or exchange

Such work fits the widely held view that trust and distrust are essentially rational, as in the encapsulated interest account in this book (Hardin 1991; 2002b, ch. 1; also see Coleman 1991, ch. 5). There are two central elements in applying a rational choice account of trust: *incentives* of the trusted to fulfill the trust, and *knowledge* to justify the truster's trust. If we are sensibly to trust you, we must know your incentives to be trustworthy in the context. Because our supposed knowledge of you and your motivations can be mistaken, and because your incentives might often not lead you to cooperate with us (you might have competing interests that trump), we typically run some risk of losing if we act cooperatively toward you. For present purposes, I will assume that knowledge problems are subsumed under such risk assessments and will not analyze them separately. They will play a significant, sometimes implicit, role in the discussions throughout.

Mutual trust

Let us begin with mutual trust, which is game theoretically more complex than the one-way trust to be discussed below, but which is better suited to establishing the role of trust in a dyadic relationship. Perhaps the prototypical case of mutual trust at the individual level involves an interaction that is part of a long sequence of exchanges between the same parties.

Each exchange is simply the resolution of a prisoner's dilemma (as in game 3.1). A sequence of exchanges is therefore an iterated prisoner's dilemma with, perhaps, some variation in the stakes at each exchange. It is not likely, in real life, to be a game of simultaneous moves but of sequential moves, in which you take the risk of doing something for me today in the expectation that I will reciprocate in some way tomorrow. The main incentive that one faces in a particular exchange in which one is trusted by the other is the potential benefit from *continuing the series of interactions*. The sanction each of us can invoke against the other is to withdraw from further interaction. In some contexts, this is a substantial sanction because there might not be a suitable alternative party for future interactions for the other person. Such iterated exchange – playing the prisoner's dilemma again and again with the same partner – does not define trust, but it is the context in which trust often arises. Indeed, reciprocal ongoing dyadic relationships commonly lead to mutual trust.

Typically, prisoner's dilemma experiments can conclude only that players do or do not cooperate under varied conditions. They cannot directly tell us what the players' motivations are. In particular, they cannot tell us that players trust or distrust each other. Some researchers introduce a prior move before the play of the prisoner's dilemma (see e.g. Yamagishi and Kakiuchi 2000). In that prior move, one or both players can alter the stakes of the game, increasing the potential winnings from cooperation while also increasing the potential losses from the other player's defection. Players who increase the stakes might be supposed to give some information about their cooperativeness, although it is not obvious what that information must say. This is a clever innovation that increases the range of behavior we have to analyze and that might, indeed, commonly reveal degrees of trust. As discussed in the concluding remarks, however, as a rule we cannot finally be sure what motivations are at stake in the playing of experimental games.

Coleman (1991: 177–80) implicitly includes the Trusted's incentives when he notes that a reciprocal trusting relationship, as in mutual trust in the iterated prisoner's dilemma, is mutually reinforcing for each Truster. Why? Because each person now has an additional incentive to be trustworthy, namely to give the other person an incentive to be trustworthy. I trust you because it is in your interest to do what I trust you to do. It is in your interest primarily because you want me to continue to be trusting and trustworthy.

One-way trust

In the one-way T-game of game 3.2, the Truster must act as though she trusts the Trusted in order to gain from their interaction. Her defection simply entails that there is no interaction, no risk, and no gain. If she acts as though she trusts Trusted, Trusted need then only act in his own interest. The game is *one-way* because it is only the Truster whose actions might depend on trusting. Trusted's action does not involve any risk. Hence, the game is genuinely one-way. In the game, the Truster makes the first move of defecting or cooperating. If she does not choose to take the risk of cooperating, the game ends with payoffs of nothing to both parties. If she takes the risk, then there is a next stage in which Trusted chooses whether to defect or cooperate, with defection being substantially more beneficial than cooperation. The play of the game ends with his choice.

If this game is played anonymously and once only, clearly Trusted's interest is to cheat; therefore Truster's interest is not to risk the initial cooperation. But actual experiments in this game show that many subjects in the role of Truster make the risky cooperative move and that many subjects in the role of Trusted reciprocate in a sense by playing cooperatively and taking a smaller gain than they could guarantee themselves (see McCabe and Smith 2002; Ahn et al. 2002). If, however, they are able to play the game repeatedly, interests change dramatically, because both can do very well over many plays of the game. If it is iterated, therefore, it turns into a game that is nearly the iterated prisoner's dilemma discussed above (it is only "nearly" the iterated prisoner's dilemma).

Note, incidentally, that the one-way T-game of game 3.2 is a three-part relation. Suppose its payoffs are in money. Truster takes a risk on Trusted with respect to a difference of $25 in the payoffs to Truster. We could make an analogous

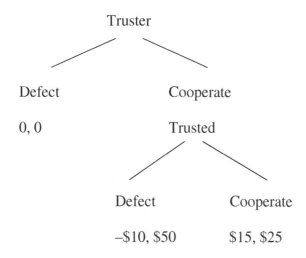

Game 3.2 One-way T-game

claim for the general T-game no matter who the parties are or what the stakes are. But, of course, it would be plausible for Truster not to take a risk on Trusted in a one-way T-game with radically higher stakes even though she would take the risk with the stakes at $25. For example, if the stakes in the lower left and right outcomes were (–$10,000, $50,001) and ($1, $40,000), as in the high stakes one-way T-game of game 3.3, we might expect Truster not to take the potentially huge risk of losing $10,000 for the chance of a gain of merely $1.

It is a great strength of the experimental protocol for the one-way T-game that it virtually forces us to be very clear about what is at issue. For example, it is very difficult to imagine a reduced analog of the one-way T-game that would represent only a two-part relation unless it allowed the payoffs to be open-ended. But then the relevant player would be unable to choose to cooperate at the first move because the loss, if the other party chose to take the noncooperative payoff, could be catastrophic; it could be analogous to the (–$10,000, $50,001) versus ($1, $40,000) outcomes. Players who understood such a game could not, if their own resources were at stake, seriously claim to think it smart to

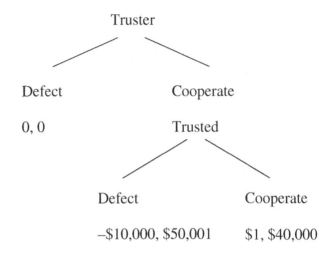

Game 3.3   One-way trust with high stakes

cooperate at the first move. Normally, iteration of a prisoner's dilemma or of a one-way T-game with the same partner might be expected to increase the level of cooperativeness. But *even if game 3.3 were iterated many times*, it seems unlikely that first movers would ever take the risk of losing so much for so little prospect of gain. After all, it would take 10,000 successful plays of the game to cover for the loss in a single unsuccessful play.

Note that the one-way T-game is in a sense only half of very many commonplace trust relations. In a mutual trust interaction, for example, both parties are at risk and both might trust or not trust and both might be trustworthy or not trustworthy. In an ongoing mutual exchange relationship, you and I might both be in a position on occasion to cheat each other. Neither of us would have the restricted role of the truster who can take a risk or not but who can do nothing else. In game 3.2 the trusted's action does not depend on trust or involve a risk. In sum, this game is not about trust on any of the three standard theories of trustworthiness.

Consider two variations on the one-way T-game: with iteration and with punishment. The one-way T-game, when repeated, has some of the qualities of the iterated prisoner's dilemma and of mutual trust. It is not a prisoner's dilemma, however, because *there is no outcome that is best for Truster that is simultaneously worst for Trusted*. The worst outcome for Trusted in any given play of the game is analogous to the noncooperation outcome (0, 0) in which, in essence, Truster prefers not to risk playing. If Trusted is the column player, the equivalent of the lower-left cell payoff (40, −30) of the prisoner's dilemma of game 3.1 is not possible. But there must be some degree of mutual trust if they are to continue playing because each time he cooperates Trusted must enhance the chance that Truster will continue to make a cooperative choice at the next play of the game. This is potentially a significant risk if the payoffs at stake are substantial. An iterated T-game can therefore tap trust; a one-shot T-game cannot.

In a punishment variant of the one-way T-game, the first mover has a chance to make a further choice after the second mover has defected, as in game 3.4 (but not if the second mover has cooperated). By choosing the payoff (−$15, $20), the first mover can punish the second mover for his defection. She has to bear a cost of the move to punish, and yet many subjects in one-way T-games accept such a cost in order to punish the second mover for defection. If there is a second round of play, *but with different partners*, having the punishment option increases or at least maintains the level of cooperation in the second round. This result follows even though the first mover in the first round de facto provides a collective good to the group of first movers on the second round, a collective good from which the first mover in the first round does not benefit (McCabe and Smith 2002). When there is no punishment available, cooperativeness unravels in repeated play with changing partners.

Many of the experimental results from T-games show that subjects play them cooperatively even when they are not to be iterated. Hence, first movers in the one-way T-game behave cooperatively in the sense of choosing to put themselves at the mercy of the second mover, who could simply choose the (−$10, $50) outcome in game 3.2. In one experiment in which the game is played a second time against a different "partner," the rate of risk-taking falls significantly with twice as many first movers choosing to terminate play imme-

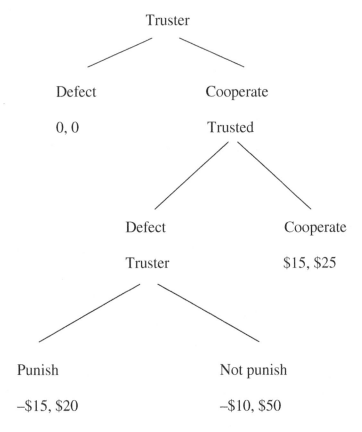

Game 3.4   One-way trust with punishment option

diately (McCabe and Smith 2002). There is no clearly ratio-nal account of why first movers should take that initial risk unless, contrary to the experimental protocol, they think that the odds are in favor of their getting a positive payoff (better than the 0 payoff they would get from not taking the risk). There is also no clearly rational account of why the second movers often choose the ($15, $25) outcome when they could do significantly better by defecting and selecting the (–$10, $50) outcome. When the game is played a second time against a different "partner," the second movers who are offered the chance of cooperating are more likely to defect. Finally, there is also no clearly rational account of why, when they are given the option of punishing the defection of second movers, as in Game 3.4, first movers do so even at cost to themselves.

Shortcomings of game experiments on trust

In a sense, the two variations – limited iteration and the punishment option – introduce more background into the play of the bare one-way T-game. The most important variant of that game would be to introduce still more background. *In the general social phenomenon of trust, much of the story is in the larger relationship that provides knowledge of others and gives them incentives to behave in trustworthy ways.* These are two of the central elements in most theories of trust, especially including the rational accounts of the encapsulated interest theory, and the normative theories. The bulk of all trust relationships may be in ongoing relationships. The game experiments deliberately ignore the relational element of real world trust relationships.

Although the one-way T-game modeled in game 3.2 represents some real world instances of choice problems, it does not include enough of the relevant payoffs to capture the sense of trust as relational in a typical field setting, as contrasted to an experimental setting. For example, so long as she has resources and relationships in the larger community, Truster might be able to inflict eventual costs on Trusted. Almost all real life games are embedded in a richer array of interactions that influence how one should choose in them. The actual motivations one faces in interactions with others are likely to be more clearly self-interested when the effects of reputation, other third-party interactions, and iteration are brought into focus, as they typically must be in real world contexts. Laboratory experiments are commonly intended to abstract from these and other societal contextual effects. Such abstraction gives them some of their clarity and resultant power. But in the T-game it blocks access to relational elements of the interactions and therefore blocks any chance of their representing trust relations.

It is implausible to say that all of these behaviors are motivated by trust as encapsulated interest, and it is also difficult to see how they are motivated by trust in any other sense. For the cooperative first movers, there appears to be either a strong normative motivation or, perhaps, a failure to grasp the strategic logic of the payoff structures. The latter possibility is suggested by the fact that, in a second round with changed partners, the level of cooperative play declines substantially, as though to imply that subjects have learned something in their prior play. Of course, they may merely be Bayesian learners who have learned that others are less likely to be cooperative than they at first assumed.

There is a standard argument about iterated prisoner's dilemma that might be thought to apply immediately to the one-way T-game. By backwards induction from what it would be rational to do on the final play of a series of prisoner's dilemmas, it is thought by some to be rational to defect on every play. The argument is this. On the last play of a fixed sequence of, say, 100 plays, there is no longer any future payoff to be secured by your cooperation in this round. Therefore you should defect. But once that is realized, the next to last play is now effectively an endgame choice, so you should defect on it also. And so on all the way back to the first play, on which you should defect. The end result of symmetric reasoning here is that we both gain nothing from our play when we might have gained, in game 3.1, close to $1,500 each.

So long as the losses at stake do not threaten bankruptcy and the potential gains are not radically smaller than the potential losses, as they are in game 3.3 (which is not a prisoner's dilemma), I think this result is simply wrong for the ordinary prisoner's dilemma (see Hardin 2003, ch. 2). But for the two-move one-way T-game, it is relatively compelling. If we assume that, as second mover, your only motivation is your own interest, then we must suppose you will defect if we give you an opportunity to take the second move. Hence, it is clearly in our interest in either game 3.2 or game 3.3 to defect at the outset in order to block you from imposing such costs on us. Suppose we understand all of this. Then, if we make the cooperative choice as first mover, it must therefore be true that we suppose you will not act merely from your own interest when you make the second move.

Cooperative play might be motivated by reasons other than trust in the encapsulated interest or normative accounts. You might act as though you trust us in order to demonstrate to us that you have faith in our morality or character, or to give us an opportunity to live up to your hopes even though we may have no direct incentive to reciprocate your action. Or you may wish not to be the kind of person who acts toward another with distrust that is not based on solid evidence. Such motivations are apt to lead to disappointment in many contexts, but they might be statistically justified in certain milieus. In particular, they might be justified in contexts in which there are rich possibilities of further interactions. In such contexts, however, interest is likely to conspire with your hopes in getting us to reciprocate. One-shot games lack any such context.

Suppose you understand the one-way T-game of game 3.2 very well and you make the cooperative choice as first mover. We might suppose you act from a relatively optimistic expectation that is not grounded in any relationship that you and we have. Indeed, as the games are typically played in the laboratory, you would not even know our identity or anything else about us, although you might reasonably suppose we are another student roughly like yourself. In a one-shot play of the game you know that we as the second mover can choose either to cooperate or to defect at no risk of retaliation from you. We therefore cannot act from an incentive grounded in our relationship. Hence, in cooperating on the first move, you are offering us a substantial benefit in the hope that we will reciprocate in making the cooperative choice as second mover.

Note that in any one-shot play of any game, such as the one-way T-game, *it is not possible to test for trust as encapsulated interest or any other standard conception of trust* because such trust requires some further relationship between the truster and the trusted. This experimental paradigm therefore rules out the standard forms that trust relationships in ordinary life take. This is, of course, a problem of one-shot games that are abstracted from even the slightest relationship between the players. More generally, the paradigm also rules out testing any theory in which trust depends on an assessment of the potentially trusted person. Such theories presume that we can somehow judge who is and who is not likely to be trustworthy because we think we know something about their motivations or incentives. In a one-shot game with an unknown other, it is impossible that I could be choosing on the basis of any such assessment of the other player. As these games are played, there is no way for the players who, as first movers, are potential cooperators to assess the trustworthiness of their partners in the game.

In addition, such games cannot tell us whether a player is trustworthy or takes a risk on the other player *out of normative commitments of some kind.* The only way to judge the choices of the players as normative is to debrief them and ask leading questions to see what might have motivated them. Merely accounting the experimental results cannot address the question. One might suppose that many players act from a strong norm of reciprocity, but the mere data on choices in one-shot games cannot tell us this. There are many possible alternative explanations of the behavior, including McCabe and Smith's error. The truth here is that first-mover cooperation in one-shot games is a mystery.

Despite their clarity in many respects, the game representations of various interactions do not clearly tell us about trust. The so-called trust game is mislabeled – it is not about trust in any meaningful sense. The broad range of potential reasons for players' choices is not narrowed to trust, self-interest, normative commitments, or any other motivation. When debriefed after participating in a one-way T-game experiment, subjects commonly speak of trust and of the other player or players as partners. We do not generally know, however, what the vernacular implications of the terms are. On the evidence of my asking dozens of people from diverse backgrounds, the vernacular meanings of trust are quite varied (see also Klitzman and Bayer 2003). Of course, one might argue that people are often lousy at giving definitions of terms that they nevertheless use very well and in apt contexts. Still, for trust we may go further and say that many people quite clearly mean different things. The variety of academic views of what trust must be is astonishing (see Hardin 2002b, ch. 3), although one might expect the philosophical and social scientific literatures to give more and odder meanings than ordinary people give. There are, after all, rewards for inventiveness in academic life. Ordinary people seem less readily inclined to invent meanings unless, perhaps, to cover the embarrassment of not knowing.

Can we say anything definitively? Perhaps only this: in a one-time play of game 3.2 against a stranger with whom one will not knowingly have any further interactions and whom one will not ever even be able to identify, it is easy to say what choice maximizes the second mover's payoff: defection. For players who defect at this point we can say that interests have almost surely trumped any other considerations that might motivate them. This is the only nearly crystal-clear claim we can make about the meaning of any choices in all of these games, although we can probably also clearly say that in the one-way T-game with high stakes (game 3.3), it is irrational for the first mover to cooperate if her own interests are the only consideration. To my knowledge, no one has had the temerity to inflict an analog of game 3.3 on real people, so that the claim here is speculative. (One might draw a clear analogy to prisoner's dilemma experiments for cases in which the payoff for cooperating when the other player defects – the so-called sucker's payoff – is extremely bad relative to the payoff from mutual cooperation or mutual defection. In such games, players need not be very risk averse to choose not to cooperate and typically they do not (Rapoport and Chammah 1965: 65).) A cooperative move by the first mover is still likely to be irrational even if other motivations might be heavily in play. We can only say that these other motivations are easily trumped by self-interest at such dramatic stakes, not that they are absent or even weak. Indeed, they might be quite strong, but a first mover with strong normative motivations might still quail in the face of a $10,000 loss as the risk for trying to obtain a trivial $1 gain.

Experimental results show that many players in the position of the second mover of game 3.2 do not make the individually maximizing choice. The chief reason must be that there is a substantial residue beyond self-interest. There is less role for such a residue in a mutual trust interaction, in which self-interest is itself likely to be adequate to motivate us. Some of the confusion over what trust is and, more generally, over what motivates individual choice in varied strategic contexts is played out in these experimental games. By implication, we are still relatively far from measuring trust experimentally in any definitive or even clear way.

The state of play

The three standard conceptions of trust are all cognitive; they make trust depend on assessments of the trustworthiness of another in the relevant circumstances. If I have reason to think you will be trustworthy, then I trust you. There are three modal conceptions of why one would be trustworthy in a particular context (I will take this last phrase for granted hereafter). You may be trustworthy for essentially rational reasons of your interests, for normative reasons, or for reasons of character or psychological disposition. That is to say, trustworthiness may be *incentive based, normatively based, or psychologically based.*

Trustworthiness that is based on psychological or normative commitments or that is based on encapsulated interests is not at issue and cannot even be tapped or elicited in most game experiments of supposed trust. Consider the normative conception (parallel claims can be made for the other two standard conceptions). In the experiments as run, the normative commitments of the potentially trusted person are not at issue when the first player decides whether to be cooperative. This is not to say that there are no choices that are driven by, say, normative commitments, but only that the commitments of the second player are usually entirely unknown to the first player because the second player and anything about that player are unknown to the first player. This usually sensible protocol for experimental games vitiates their use in studying trust because these commitments are specifically what define standard normative accounts of trust, in which the normatively motivated trustworthiness of some people is used to explain the trust that others have in them.

Standard theories of trust that make trust depend on the normative or other commitments of the trusted cannot be tested by experimental games that are played in ignorance of who the other player is. That is the way the vast bulk of experiments on the one-way T-game are played. The standard conceptions of trust all require a specific judgment of whether the other person is trustworthy (in a few experiments, there is at least iterated play to reveal much about the two players to each other; see, for example, Coye and Cook 2004). In the standard normative theories of trust, we trust you because, for example, we think you have a moral commitment to being trustworthy (such as following a norm of reciprocity) or we think you have a psychological disposition to be trustworthy. The first mover in a one-shot, one-way T-game with no information on the other player cannot judge that the other player has such a normative commitment or follows such a norm. Play in these games might partially differentiate those among second movers who act from a norm of reciprocity or fairness from those who do not.

Again, the protocols for many experimental games are explicitly intended to *block giving the first mover any information about the possible motivations of the second player.* In real world contexts, such devices as reading another's face or actions in another context might give us information about a potential second mover and lead us to presume that that person has a moral commitment or is likely to follow a norm of reciprocity, as in the account of social intelligence in Yamagishi and Kakiuchi (2000). Even in the highly restrictive conditions of most game experiments ostensibly on trust, the second player does have one piece of information about the first player – whether the first player acted cooperatively. The second player therefore could act from a normative commitment or norm of reciprocity in response to the first player's action (see Ostrom 2002; Ahn et al. 2002). Your following a norm of reciprocity makes you relatively *trustworthy to those who know you follow such a norm.* Richer debriefing of subjects in these games might suggest that they are normatively motivated in various ways. But the mere payoff structure of the games and the bald choices cannot tell us why a second player cooperates.

In the current literature on trust, the only view that could bring normative commitments into the first player's decision in a one-shot, one-way T-game is the view that trusting is itself morally required. Almost no one argues for this view (exceptions are Hertzberg 1988 and perhaps Uslaner 2002; see further, Hardin 2002b, ch. 3). Indeed, this view cannot generally be correct because, for example, as noted earlier, it would be immoral and harmful to trust anyone and everyone to babysit for one's infant. Trust therefore cannot be strictly moral or morally required. In general, almost all the standard theories of trust, whether incentive based or normatively based, are inherently theories of trustworthiness, which can be morally motivated, as it clearly seems to be in some cases.

Fehr et al. (2002: 521) note rightly that experimental results are "valid if there is good reason to believe that the experimental environment, under which the results have been generated, captures essential elements of naturally occurring environments." They then run experiments on supposed trust that use one-way T-games played entirely anonymously. This specifically rules out any relational elements between the players and therefore rules out any chance of testing for any of the standard conceptions of trust. Fehr et al. correct in part for this failing by using survey questionnaires to get at their players' motives. Unfortunately, they find that "none of the survey measures of trust are good predictors of trustworthiness in the experiment" (2002: 534; also see Glaeser et al. 2000). Perhaps this should come as no surprise because the experiments do not actually map any standard account of trust and cannot do so. So let us turn to survey research on trust.

Survey Research

There are two issues to which survey research on trust is typically addressed. One of these is levels of interpersonal trust, and the other is levels of so-called trust in government. Principal attention in the past decade has been given to the second of these issues. Let us address both in turn, beginning with studies of interpersonal trust.

The point of wanting more trust in personal relations is that trusting the trustworthy eases the way to cooperative social relations. But it is hard to see just why more trust per se is wanted. We want As to trust Bs to do Xs (Hardin 1991, 2002b). When we think of the problem in this unpacked form, we immediately focus on specific devices to get the Bs to do Xs – that is, *on the trustworthiness of the Bs*. For example, the massive system of contract enforcement in any flourishing market society serves agents who do not genuinely trust each other with respect to anything in particular, who, indeed, need not even know each other at all well enough to be "trusting" without backing from the law. Yet, the system enables them to enter into very complex cooperative relations that are mutually beneficial. The very specific confidence to comply with a legal contract is grounded in the system of contract enforcement. Or, as is true in many ongoing business relations, it is iterated or repeated interaction that gives the parties an incentive to behave well in this moment because they want the relationship to continue in future moments. For example, if I regularly supply your firm with some input and you object that the quality of one of my shipments is poor, it will be in my interest, if possible, to make the shipment right independently of the terms of our contractual agreement – because I will want to keep your business. I could insist on the letter of the contract, which may include a caveat emptor (let the buyer beware) clause. But then you might find an alternative supplier for your future needs. And in any case I will want to maintain a reputation for reliability if I am to attract other buyers of my goods.

Current writings commonly focus on trust as somehow the relevant variable in explaining differences across cases of successful cooperation. Typically, however, the crucial variable is the *trustworthiness of those who are to be trusted or relied upon.* If popular assessments of government, as measured by responses to vague questionnaire items – such as "How much do you trust government to do what is right?" – suggest declining confidence in government, we should similarly suppose that the problem to be explained is declining performance or responsiveness of government. If we think there are problems inherent in declining trust, we might attempt to address these by encouraging more trust or, alternatively, securing greater trustworthiness. Clearly, if a person, such as your child, were distrustful, you would want to encourage that person to be more trusting only if trust would be justified, that is to say, if the people to be trusted would likely be trustworthy. If we can tell at all accurately from our experience with particular people that they are apt to be trustworthy in certain circumstances, we will then trust them as much as judgment of their trustworthiness merits.

For measures of trust, there are two major survey instruments in the United States, and related instruments in many other advanced democracies. There are also the World Values surveys, which are cross-cultural (as were the early surveys of five nations by Almond and Verba 1965). It is the systematic quality and the decades-long repetition of some of these survey instruments that make them very influential in general and that have given the American worry about declining trust its great impetus. We are commonly afflicted with worries that somehow things are not as good as they were before. But in this realm, there are many good reasons to suppose that much of life has got significantly better in many of the nations in which there are worries about decline.

Interpersonal trust

Here are the questions used by NORC (the National Opinion Research Center at the University of Chicago) in the General Social Survey (GSS) for the assessment of levels of *interpersonal trust*:

1   Do you think most people would try to take advantage of you, or would they try to be fair?
2   Would you say that most of the time people try to be helpful, or that they are mostly looking out for themselves?
3   Generally speaking, would you say that most people can be trusted, or that you can't be too careful dealing with people?

As with the experimental games research, the most striking feature of survey work on interpersonal trust is how a-theoretical it is – as is evident from these questions. The notion of trust is left completely untheorized. It is the respondents, not the social scientists, who implicitly define it. Yet, there are many studies of actual people's views that are based on in-depth interviews, rather than merely responses to survey items. Many of these studies suggest that vernacular views are enormously varied. People give very different accounts of what they mean by trust (see the extraordinary variety of views in Klitzman and Bayer 2003). Ordinary people are not alone in this liability; there is perhaps an even larger variety of academic views on what trust "is" (see an account in Hardin 2002b, ch. 3).

Most of the survey research on trust implicitly assumes that the notion of trust has a commonly understood meaning. It therefore *does not test* for different conceptions or theories of trust. If survey subjects use their own perhaps quite varied vernacular senses of trust, and the survey analyses lump all of these together as simply "trust," then we *cannot readily use the extant data to test any particular theory or conception of trust.* Unless we can show that responses in the vernacular correlate with responses to some more articulated account of trust, we generally cannot be sure what the survey responses mean.

Glance back at the GSS questions. Immediately, one can see a great merit and a great demerit of these questions. The great merit is that they fairly overtly ask for judgments of the *trustworthiness* of others. The great demerit is their conceptual vacuity in the sense that the questions do not differentiate varied conceptions of trust and they do not address or acknowledge the relational character of actual trust. They do not differentiate varied categories of people whom one would be more or less likely to trust, and they do not differentiate different objects of trust ranging from reciprocating minor favors to fulfilling major, very costly promises. The questions generally ask about trusting everyone or most people, implicitly with respect to anything at all. In the formula A trusts B with respect to X, both B and X in the survey instruments often implicitly roam over the ranges of everyone and everything. No sane person trusts everyone equally and with respect to any and every level of risk. It is a merit of game experiments on trust that they do not allow such vacuous generality of what X can be.

Hence, either the surveyors ask for insane responses, or respondents to these surveys have to create their own universe of people and objects to which they then apply the questions. You might narrow the population down from everyone to merely those with whom you deal, that is, to the category that would fit trust as a relational concept. Others might narrow it to those whom they might encounter on the sidewalks and in the shops of their city. Perhaps people narrow the field today in relatively different ways from how they narrowed it several decades ago. Who can possibly know what the responses to such ill-defined questions tell us about actual levels of trust or about trends in trust over time in any well-defined context?

There are many surveys done for varied purposes that do make some of these differentiations possible. Some surveys differentiate the objects to which they then apply the trust questions (e.g., see Gibson 2001). The objects may be various professional and employment groups and officers of various levels and agencies of government. But the bulk of the work that worries about declining levels of trust in some societies is based very heavily on the massive samples answering standard surveys such as the GSS with their underspecified questions. Perhaps there are meaningful senses in which there is declining trust. But at the same time there is, as noted in chapter 1, substantial reason to suppose that our relationships have become both more varied and more numerous over recent decades. Hence, we individually seem to trust more people than ever, although the other side of this coin is that we must also distrust more people than ever. The interesting phenomenon is that we have more relationships than ever, so that any relational concept, such as trust, is put to greater and more varied tests today than several decades ago. Perhaps we should think this is a good thing, not a sign of decay and decline. The expansion of relational and life opportunities has been not merely good for many of us but, indeed, wonderful. We would never return to the world of Bodo – or even that of our grandparents.

Trust in government

Turn now to debates over declining confidence in government in some advanced democracies, notably including Canada, the United Kingdom, and the United States. Why is such decline happening? Does it matter? And, finally, is it even meaningful? Much of the vast contemporary literature on this issue treats the declining confidence as a matter of declining trust. This is a misguided, a-theoretical use of "trust," as explained below, and I will speak only of declining confidence. In chapter 8 I propose answers to these questions – answers that make sense only if the issue is one of confidence rather than trust – and I offer speculations on their implications for democracy. Although there are probably many causal factors in any social change this grand and widespread, I will focus on a related pair of changes in the nature of the issues governments in the advanced democracies face. Their historical focus on economic issues – whether to use central planning and distribution or to rely on the market – has largely been settled in a remarkable change of world conditions over the past two decades or so. At the same time, the range of policy issues at stake has grown more diverse and technically more complex and therefore evidently harder to handle successfully.

Here is the battery of four questions that constitute the trust scale for *trust in government* in the National Election Studies (NES) surveys:

1 How much of the time do you think you can trust the government in Washington to do what is right – just about always, most of the time, or only some of the time?
2 Would you say the government is pretty much run by a few big interests looking out for themselves or that it is run for the benefit of all the people?
3 Do you think that people in the government waste a lot of money we pay in taxes, waste some of it, or don't waste very much of it?
4 Do you think that quite a few of the people running the government are crooked, not very many are, or do you think hardly any of them are crooked?

These NES survey items were originally proposed as a cynicism scale. That scale was devised in an effort to understand the low levels of participation in democratic politics in the United States, where the turnouts even for quadrennial presidential elections were typically about 60 percent or less when the scale was introduced around 1960. The cynicism scale was seen as a measure of the general attitude toward government. Cynicism is essentially the belief that others are motivated only by self-interest. Although cynicism is not an analog of distrust, most of those very cynical about government might reasonably be expected to say they distrust it or its officials.[12]

Inverting the cynicism scale to make it a measure of trust in government, as is commonly done, makes much less sense. Mere lack of cynicism is not sufficient to define trust. I could suppose that my government is motivated not by the self interest of its officials but by commitments that are ideological, religious, moralistic, or hostile to my particular group while supportive of various other groups, or that it is driven by a stupid economic theory. In all these cases, even though I would not have a cynical view of the government, I would deeply distrust it as working contrary to my interests. Although only the second and the fourth items in the cynicism scale are strictly about cynicism, the questions in the scale seem to be a fair guide to cynicism, hence to distrust. But they are little guide at all to trust on any of the three standard conceptions of trust.[13] Only the first item might tap one of the standard conceptions of trust, that which grounds trust in the moral commitments of the potentially trusted.

In sum, the opposite of cynicism is confidence that the motivations of government and its agents are not exclusively self-interested. Such confidence is far less than trust, although it is a part of trust. There are many ways not to be cynical, not all of which entail a judgment of trustworthiness, although cynicism about government's motivations does entail a judgment that it is untrustworthy. The inverted cynicism scale is therefore not a trust scale.

How should we interpret responses to various standard questions on trust in government? It is not plausible to treat them as articulately responsive to any reflective sense of trust, of what trust is and how it works. But *they presumably do reflect people's real experiences.* They are implicit claims about the trustworthiness or reliability of relevant others. Again, if there are changes over time or differences across contexts in the level of "trust" that people express in responding to the survey questions, we should look to changes or differences in the behavior of those who are supposedly trusted to explain why they are trusted less or more. Hence, if confidence in government is declining, we should address that problem by enhancing government's competence, if possible.

Conceptual issues Before turning to explanations and implications, let us address three conceptual issues of the uses and abuses of the terminology of trust in this context. First, is trust in government analogous to trust in another person, or is it a very different notion? The answer clearly is that it is not analogous to personal trust most of the time (Hardin 1998b). The nature of a personal relationship involving trust is far richer and more directly reciprocal than the citizen's relationship to government. It is a genuinely, even deeply relational phenomenon. Hence, we should not speak of citizens' trust in government but of their *confidence* in government. I will therefore speak generally of confidence in government, but it should be clear that this notion is a partial analog of trust, as spelled out below. That is what licenses the vernacular use of the term even in the loose context of the citizen's relation to government. But it is only a partial analog and much of the force of claims of trust does not apply to claims of confidence. For example, for many writers, declining trust suggests a normative problem. Declining confidence does not so readily provoke normative concerns.

The second issue, already raised in chapter 2, is that we should be concerned with trustworthiness rather than with trust (Hardin 1996), because if we wish to induce changes somewhere, it is most likely changes in trustworthiness that we want. If there have been changes in citizens' propensity to trust government, the first supposition we should make is that those changes are rooted in changes in the perceived trustworthiness of government or other actors in our lives and not in changes in our trustingness, credulity, or basic psychological make-up (this thesis is spelled out in chapter 8; see further, Newton and Norris 2000). A secular trend in human psychology is very unlikely.

Finally, we should recognize that trust involves an expectation that the trusted has both the right motivations and the competence to fulfill the trust. Unless there is good evidence to suppose politicians have become less honorably motivated in recent decades, we should probably focus our attention on problems of *competence*, not of motivation.[14] Some chapters here do not focus much on competence because it is not a crucial issue for their discussions. In the analysis of declining confidence in government, it may well be the crucial issue and we will need to address it. This is an interesting fact because reduced trust in other individuals over time must typically turn on motivational rather than competence issues, although there are exceptions, such as declining trust in someone who loses short-term memory.

There is one other conceptual issue (to be addressed in chapter 4): the nature of social capital, which is thought by some to be declining in the United States. If so, its decline might contribute to the loss of confidence in government at least in the United States, although not likely in most other advanced democracies, some of which recently had far worse governments than they have today, and none of which has the panoply of spontaneous groups exhibited in the US since the visit of Tocqueville.

Governmental decline?   With these conceptual issues out of the way, we can turn to explaining the apparent decline in confidence in government, which shows up in surveys in several of the advanced democracies. I will assume that responses to survey questions on trust are evidence of belief that governmental performance is failing in some way relative to past performance. I will focus on one explanation of declining confidence in government, which will be discussed below in the section on "Competence and motivation." Its consequences for politics and government will then be discussed in chapter 8.

Government today may be neither more nor less competent than it was two generations ago, but its agenda may have changed in ways that make contemporary governments *seem* less competent to handle the problems they face. Government may not be less competent in the absolute, but it seems less competent relative to the problems it faces. In particular, the once relatively simple economic conflict over whether to have central planning or to let the market run has largely been settled in favor of the market (chapter 8). The issues that now dominate political agendas in the advanced democracies are much less systematically related than the former economic issues were, and they are often technically complex and essentially beyond popular understanding. But failure in dealing with them is often not beyond popular understanding. Hence, the governments increasingly seem to be maladept.

Discussions of trust have become commonplace in the analysis of governmental responsiveness and the attitudes of citizens toward government (Bianco 1994), in efforts to understand differential economic success across societies (Fukuyama 1995), and in discussions of the relations between clients and various professionals, such as doctors (Barber 1983). It is common in these discussions to suppose that trust is essentially good because it has good consequences and, hence, to suppose that generally higher levels of trust in government would be good. Many recent, well-received works make strong claims for the great value of trust, and at least implicitly therefore for the value of enhancing trust (Luhmann 1980; Putnam 1995a, 1995b; Fukuyama 1995; Uslaner 2002). If we wish to understand the role of trust in society, however, we must get beyond the flaccid – and often wrong – assumption that trust is simply good. This supposition must be heavily qualified, because trusting the malevolent or the radically incompetent can be foolish and often even grossly harmful.

Even if trust is important in society, however, it does not follow that trust in government is important or even meaningful, although countless polls now address supposedly declining trust in government and other institutions. Much of the apparent shock value of such studies depends on the presumption that trusting government is roughly analogous to trusting a person. For the most part, this is an incoherent assumption. To say that we trust you suggests several things. First, we expect you to do certain things. Second and third, we think you have the motivation and the capacity to do those things. And finally, if our trust is to be specifically of you, we think your motivation is to do those things because they benefit us, not merely because you might have wanted to do them anyway or were being paid by somebody to do them independently of the fact that they interest us.

In French there is no neat equivalent of the English verb to trust. The nearest is "avoir confiance," to have confidence. The French term is apt for what most English speakers presumably mean when they say such things as "I trust that the sun will rise tomorrow, as always." Here, the use of "trust" is otiose. It adds nothing beyond saying that I expect the sun to rise or that I understand the physics of the sun's rising daily. Of course, the vernacular allows for the use of trust in such trivializing ways, but we should not find much of interest about such "trust." It is similarly trivializing to say of most people that they trust government or some government official whom they personally do not know or have a relationship with, rather than that they expect the government and its officials to do certain things.[15]

Could typical citizens meaningfully trust government in the way that they do trust their friends and other associates? In general, no. For us to trust you means that we have to know a fair amount about you. Our knowledge might be wrong and we might therefore wrongly trust or distrust you. But in general, for us to trust you we must believe your motivations toward us are to serve our interests, broadly conceived, with respect to the issues at stake. We could believe this if we believe any of the following things. First, you value our relationship enough to want to maintain it, so that you will want to fulfill the trust we place in you, as in the encapsulated interest conception of trust. Second, you value us enough to include our interests in your own, as a parent, lover, or close friend might do.[16] Third, you have such strong moral commitments to, say, fidelity that you will want to fulfill our trust.[17] Or fourth, you have a strong psychological disposition to be the kind of person who is trustworthy.

Only the first of these could plausibly be attributed to government officials in general (although some officials might want us to believe that the second fits them). But even it asks too much in the sense that few of us can know many government officials and their commitments well enough to judge whether they actually value their relationships with us. Elected officials want our votes; bureaucrats want even less from us. Conceptually it is technically possible that someone might have trust in this sense in government or, rather, a government agency or official, although epistemologically that would be very demanding because it would require vastly too much knowledge (Hardin 1998b, 2000, 2002a).

At present, to my knowledge, no elected government official knows me at all. Some have met me but I suspect that they have long since forgotten me (some have long since forgotten their mothers). It is implausible that any of them is motivated by concern for my interests. True, many of them want my vote and the votes of people like me. But in this, they may be merely self-serving and opportunistic and they may as soon not serve my interests when that will help them get elected. If I trust them in the trivializing vernacular sense above, that is what I trust them to do: to act relatively opportunistically. It would be silly for me to say I trust those officials the way I trust many of my associates in many parts of my life.

Because there is no evidence that anyone actually trusts government in the ways they actually do trust some persons, and because it is very difficult to see how they sensibly could, again it makes better sense analytically to speak not of declining trust in government but of declining confidence. We should therefore evidently read the massive survey research data on the matter to be about confidence, not trust, in government. Being confident of an agency might be epistemologically easy as merely a generalization from its past behavior without any genuine knowledge about anyone in the agency or about their motivations toward us.

Finally, there is a widely held view that government needs the trust of citizens if it is to work well. For example, Richard Rose (1994: 18) writes, "Trust is a necessary condition for both civil society and democracy." Adam Seligman (1997: 6) makes the somewhat restricted but still grand claim that generalized trust is *necessary* for the workings of civil society. William Gamson (1968: 43) says that the loss of the trust of citizens "is the loss of system power, the loss of a generalized capacity for authorities to commit resources to attain collective goals." The view is perhaps a variant of the Durkheim–Parsons claim that social order rests on shared normative commitments (Parsons [1937] 1968: 89–94). This is not the place to quarrel with that extraordinary and virtually unresearchable claim. But the more recent view of the role of trust can only make sense if by trust is meant essentially confidence and, perhaps, some element of cooperativeness – perhaps nothing stronger than acquiescence (Hardin

1999c). Government might need this much if it is to gain citizen compliance with sometimes hard laws, such as those on taxes and conscription, although there are few to no direct data on motivations of citizens in such contexts (Levi 1997). If government needs trust in the strong sense in which our personal relationships need trust and trustworthiness to prosper as well as they do, then government has been failing us throughout the history of modern democracy and virtually must fail, because most citizens cannot trust government that way.

Competence and motivation   Recall that trust has two quite distinct dimensions: competence to perform what one is trusted to do and motivation to perform. The dimensions of competence and motivation are independent. If we wish to understand the decline in confidence in government, therefore, we must separate these two considerations and get separate assessments of them. Judging the motivations or commitments of government agents may often be difficult, but we might suppose there is little reason to think such agents are more venal or untrustworthy in their commitments today than they were a generation or two past. If so, then declining confidence in government might largely reflect governmental failure.

Why might governmental performance be in decline? The tasks that government takes on may have grown more complex and difficult in our time. Yet the capabilities of government agencies and agents may not have grown to match the increased burden they face. World War II required massive mobilization and, hence, great demands on government. The war in Vietnam required less massive mobilization but, in some ways, greater demands on the military, because the nature of that war was radically more complex than that of the war in Europe and the Pacific. The apparent competence of the military in World War II may have produced fairly high levels of confidence in government, while the apparent incompetence of the military in Vietnam may have produced low levels of confidence. Recall the quip, after the first Iraq war was over but while the war in Bosnia still raged, that the American military does deserts but not mountains and jungles. This adage makes precisely the point that judgments of competence depend on the ease of fulfillment of tasks. We might, of course, adjust our judgments of competence to match the differing difficulty of accomplishing various tasks. But we might be poor at doing that and the citizens of any nation might be inclined to judge their government competent or incompetent according to how well it masters the tasks it actually faces, not according to how well it could master any particular task.

Some of the changing attitude to government and its agents may therefore be structural. For the United States, the war on poverty, the war in Vietnam, and the war on drugs all sounded simple enough for a nation with a long history of winning wars. But all failed fairly conspicuously and many citizens may simply have concluded that a government that was once relatively competent has turned into one that is relatively incompetent. Failures of massive welfare systems in other advanced democratic nations similarly suggest government incompetence. Indeed, the share of government in the national economies of many nations may be distressing to many of their citizens. Similarly the banking disasters of the United States and Japan suggest remarkable incompetence in an arena in which government was ostensibly engaged in careful oversight.

Concluding Remarks

If experiments on trust are to give us measures of trust as encapsulated interest or of any other standard conception of trust, they will have to include more of the knowledge and motivations of the players. For the encapsulated interest view, they will have to include some analog of the background that gives people the incentives they normally have to be trustworthy. One-way and one-shot game experiments are generally too spare to give or to tap any such incentives. Indeed, none of the results from such experiments can help us test for the encapsulated-interest (including the thick-relationships), psychological-disposition, or moral-commitment views of trustworthiness. Most of the experiments could accurately be called models of very thin relationships, as in no relationship beyond the immediate interaction. To test any of the standard views requires more information to the players – at a minimum it requires information from iteration.

To test views that trust depends on an assessment of the character or moral commitments of the trusted, the experiments will have to allow some assessment of these. Playing games completely in ignorance of who the other is cannot tap motivations grounded specifically in the character of the other. *The design of most so-called trust experiments precludes testing any of the standard theories, either interest based or normative, of why people trust.* T-games as played do not and cannot model trust. It is remarkable that the vast body of experimental games and most survey research have been driven by no theoretical conception of trust beyond a seat-of-the-pants sense that we must all know what it is. All of the standard theories are grounded in the truster's knowledge or judgment of the motivations, character, or commitments of the trusted, and many of the experiments deliberately exclude such knowledge for the first movers. If the standard theories are compelling, what we need is a trustworthiness game rather than the T-game. Iterated prisoner's dilemma or iterated versions of the T-game provide de facto tests of the encapsulated interest theory. Debriefing seems, to date, the main way experimenters have found to assess normative accounts.

Finally, repetition is not strictly iteration in many of the experiments ostensibly on trust (such as those of McCabe and Smith 2002), because it is not repetition by the same partners. Play in some of the experiments suggests that subjects fairly quickly learn or try to figure out what is at issue, so that first plays may tell us very little about trust, trustworthiness, self-interest, or *any other* motivation. Rather, they may chiefly tell us that many subjects do not immediately understand the problems of strategic interaction and cooperation, as modeled by the games.

Unlike the findings from experimental games, survey results can be based on questions that are vague and even glib and can therefore confuse what is at issue. It is not the respondents to such surveys who are responsible for the glibness, it is the surveyors. For example, the most direct question about trust in the long-running General Social Survey is: "Generally speaking, would you say that most people can be trusted, or that you can't be too careful dealing with people?" This question appears to make trust a two-part relation, which is to say it is not dependent on the sizes of gains or losses from successful or failed cooperation. But surely if the payoffs were stipulated as in the one-way T-game with high stakes in game 3.3, the frequency of positive responses would fall radically. Hence, respondents must take the survey question as elliptical and they are forced to give elliptical answers. Anyone who responds to a question this vague must implicitly restrict its scope to a less significant range of possibilities than those of game 3.3. One of the beauties of the experimental paradigm (as represented by many contributions to Ostrom and Walker 2002) is that it imposes sharpness. An experimental protocol for trust must specify players (at least two) and payoffs. Hence, it virtually requires treating trust as a three-part relation (although see further comments below).

This survey question is sometimes taken to be two-part in another sense. It is supposed that it stipulates only one party, as though to say I trust virtually everyone or at least certain general categories of people (all Americans, all blacks, all women, all children). But the question must be taken as elliptical and incomplete in this sense as well. If we fill in categories and further stipulate characteristics of the individuals in the categories, we must surely again find that respondents differentiate their responses accordingly, perhaps to a very articulate extent, as in surveys that stipulate whether the "most people" whom one does or does not trust are randomly selected from the population or are the people one knows (see e.g. Gibson 2001). Typically, experiments with the one-way T-game similarly also leave open who the second party is, because players usually do not know who their "partners" are. At best they presumably suspect that these "partners" are others much like themselves, so that they are playing against someone from a fairly specific category. Ironically, the game experiments provide the degrees of constraint on the sizes of gains and losses from successful or failed cooperations that the survey items need to give them relevant sharpness. Some of the trust questions focus, rightly, on the trustworthiness of the other player rather than simplistically on trust.

Both of the current empirical research programs on trust are largely misguided. The T-games, as played, miss the possibilities of reliance on assessments of the other's motivations through iterated interaction or through reputational effects. Therefore, the game experiments do not elicit or measure anything resembling ordinary trust relations; and their findings are basically irrelevant to the modeling and assessment of trust and trustworthiness. The only thing that relates the so-called trust game (game 3.2) to trust is its name, which is wrong and misleading. Survey questions currently in wide use are radically unconstrained. They therefore force subjects to assume the relevant degrees of constraint, such as how costly the risk of failed cooperation would be. It seems unlikely that all respondents assume the same degrees of these things.

In sum, therefore, there is relatively little to learn about trust from these two massive research programs. Without retuning their protocols to address standard conceptions of trust, they cannot contribute much to understanding trust as we generally know it, and they cannot play a very constructive role in explaining social behavior, institutions, or social and political change. These are distressing conclusions because both these enterprises have been enormous and in many ways they have been carried out with admirable care.

4
Social Capital and Trust

In his nine-month tour of the young United States in 1831–2, Alexis de Tocqueville ([1835 and 1840] 1966) observed a staggering number and variety of groups that were spontaneously organized for uncounted purposes. He noted that there was nothing comparable in the old world of Europe. He saw this group activity as both the basis and the result of a popular democracy in which there was equality of political participation without respect to status (for adult white males). His observation has recently been turned into the view that such groups constitute a form of social capital on which democracy and government can draw. In the view of some, this richness of capital is now in decline and therefore democracy and popular government are at risk. There is a degree of myopic Americanism in such a conclusion because European democracies seem to work quite well without so great a tradition of group activities. But we might still conclude that the ostensible decline in trust – or, better, confidence – in government that shows up in surveys somehow turns on a correlated or even causal decline in social capital.

According to a typical definition, social capital is "features of social organization, such as trust, norms, and networks, that can improve the efficiency of society by facilitating coordinated action" (Putnam 1993: 167). Although the term "social capital" itself is a recent coinage, concern with the things that have been discussed under that label has been long-standing in sociological theory.[18] James Coleman has been the most influential proponent of viewing these as systematically related. In his first treatment of social capital, he discusses it as follows:

> Social capital is defined by its function. It is not a single entity but a variety of different entities, with two elements in common: they all consist of some aspect of social structures, and they facilitate certain actions of actors – whether persons or corporate actors – within the structure. Like other forms of capital and human capital, social capital is not completely fungible but may be specific to certain activities. A given form of social capital that is valuable in facilitating certain actions may be useless or even harmful for others. (Coleman 1988: S98; also see Coleman 1991: 302–4)

In his applications of the idea of social capital, Coleman considers the lower-level structures of ongoing relationships, family, work groups, and so forth (Coleman 1991: 300–21, 361–3, 590–3, 595–6). These structures enable us, as individuals or corporate actors, to do many things, including cooperate successfully with each other in manifold ways. They also often enable us to trust each other by protecting our relationships from abuse. A very clear use of the term is Jane Jacobs's (1961: 138) network of social relations that make daily life in an urban environment work well. Or, as Coleman (1991: 304) says, social capital is embodied in relations among individuals. As is trust, social capital is relational.

Other recent users of the term typically do not define it specifically but rather refer to instances of it or give very general characterizations of it. John Brehm and Wendy Rahn (1997: 999) define social capital as "the web of cooperative relationships between citizens that facilitates resolution of collective action problems." Francis Fukuyama shares this general view with Brehm, Rahn, and Putnam. Of these scholars, he gives the loosest and most general statement of what social capital is: "the ability of people to work together for common purposes in groups and organizations" (Fukuyama 1995: 10). (For earlier discussions, see Ostrom and Ahn 2003.)

For yet a third vision of the workings of social capital, one way to read the growing literature on the relational theory of contract (and other) law is as an account of the ways social capital can enable us to cooperate without the use of the sanctions of the law as much more than a backdrop to protect us against the worst abuses we might experience (Macneil 1980; Macauley 1963; also see Williamson 1985). Hence, social capital (in various ongoing relationships) can be used to displace institutional capital (legal institutions) that is putatively less effective or efficient, at least at the margin or for matters that would not be costly enough to justify the use of courts and lawyers. Similarly, in much of the neo-institutional account of the success of firms, the focus is on the informal devices of social capital that displace or augment the formal devices of hierarchical control (Williamson 1975, 1981).

For the political scientists Brehm, Fukuyama, Putnam, Rahn, and others, the interest in social capital "is motivated primarily by the linkage between levels of social capital and collective outcomes; high levels of social capital appear to be crucial for such measures of collective well-being as economic development, effective political institutions, low crime rates, and lower incidences of other social problems such as teen pregnancy and delinquency" (Brehm and Rahn 1997: 1000). They focus on trust, norms, and networks, all of which seem to be at the individual level. But, for them, the central concern is with how individual-level factors *facilitate the working of institutions*, including the whole of government. Hence, at least initially the view of Putnam and the political scientists is strikingly different from that expressed by Coleman in the passage quoted above. They tend to reverse Coleman's characterization, in which various instances of social capital all *"facilitate certain actions of actors."* Although he also mentions corporate actors as beneficiaries of social capital, in Coleman's actual instances of applying the notion, the function of social capital is to enable individuals (and groups of individuals) to achieve things they could not otherwise achieve so well, as in the examples he gives of student political groups, doctor–patient relations, neighborhood child care, and a Cairo bazaar (Coleman 1991: 302–4).

For political scientists, it is social capital at the individual level that allows groups and societies to manage at the highest collective level. In particular, individual-level social capital contributes to the working of the institutions of government and the performance of the economy, as is suggested by the titles of works by Brehm and Rahn (1997), Fukuyama (1995), and Putnam (1993). The causal relation is a bit loose and, indeed, it is chiefly merely asserted from various correlations. The main correlation for Putnam and others, who are worried about the possible decline of government effectiveness over time, is a putative and simultaneous decline in so-called generalized trust (the tendency to trust everyone, including strangers) and in trusting government (a vast collection of strangers) over the past few decades in the United States. The main, somewhat loose, correlation for Fukuyama (1995; see also Hollis 1998) is between cross-societal differences in general trusting and in economic performance.

Causally, the main difference between the political scientists and Coleman is the direction of their causal arrows. Coleman's arrow generally goes from the level of social relations (that ground social capital) to the individual level. For the political scientists the causal arrow goes from the individual level to the institutional level, as though to say that individuals are part of government's capital. The difference can be exemplified by the nature of the concern with trust in the two visions. For Coleman, various relationships enable individuals to trust each other; for the others, individual-level trust enables institutions to work well. In many ways, Coleman's is the better move.

Hence, under the rubric of social capital, we seemingly cover several quite varied and often amorphous *causal relations*: from the effects of lower-level social interactions that facilitate individual achievements for Coleman, from individual-level trust to social institutions and other collective-level outcomes in the recent work of political scientists, and the displacement of some institutional-level devices by individual-level relationships in the relational theory of law. Still others see social capital at work in facilitating the relations between organizations (e.g. Leeuw 1997: 484). Notably missing from the list is the *effects of institutions on lower-level interactions* (see Cook, Hardin, and Levi 2005). The use of social capital is sometimes seen as an alternative to the use of institutions in achieving cooperation.

Despite the variations, this recent wave of work on social capital may be one of the most interesting and potentially most important moves in recent social theory. And its multi-faceted and possibly even incoherent character might reflect nothing more than the usual effort to grapple with a new idea before getting it nailed down and making it finally useful in our explanations. Much of the variation in the discussions can be clarified easily and, if it is, the concepts at issue become much more useful to our understanding of relevant causal effects.

In the discussions below, I will sometimes use the term *interpersonal capital* for the general category of the various things Coleman and the political scientists call social capital. That is a more informative label for what they mean, which is mainly the relationships with others that enable us to do various things. Rich relationships are part of such capital, but whether other particular things, such as norms or trust, belong in interpersonal capital will turn on explanatory or causal understandings of these. Including them merely by definition makes using the concept relatively messy when, in Coleman's case, that concept is used to explain trust and, in the case of Putnam and others, it is supposed to include trust.[19]

To keep discussion more precisely focused, I will also more specifically refer to *organizational* and *network* capital rather than the more inclusive and amorphous social capital. It is probably a mistake to treat social capital as an aspect of or necessarily a product of trust. Network, organizational, institutional, and the more general social capital are resources that can enable us to accomplish goals and to cooperate even in contexts in which we do not trust. A vast variety of social devices, including institutions, norms, and so forth, enable us to cooperate even in the absence of trust (this is the general thesis of Cook, Hardin, and Levi 2005). Perhaps this is the chief value of social capital: *it substitutes for trust relationships.* For those who are part of a network, the relevant network capital might depend on trust as encapsulated interest from iterated interactions and reputational effects. But you might be able to mobilize a network in which you are not a regular participant, so that you can use the network to further your purposes. You are part of the social capital in the first case, and you merely have access to it in the second case (see further, Cook, Hardin, and Levi 2005, ch. 5).

Another mistake is the tendency to speak of social capital as though it were a particular kind of thing that has generalized value, as money very nearly does (Portes and Sensenbrenner 1993). But it must vary in the sense that what is functional in one context may not be in another. Consider an example. Teenagers network in two quite different ways (Heimer 1990). In many communities, they come together by coordinating on a spot – for example, the local square where there might be cafés or other points of teenage interest, the local playground, or, in American cities, the outdoor basketball court of a local school. In other communities, especially including relatively well-off and suburban communities, they come together by making deliberate arrangements over the telephone. Perhaps both groups create and use a kind of social or network capital, but the kinds are quite different. Moreover the skills involved in one kind might be more widely useful. In particular, the deliberate organization via telephone calls might be very good practice for the kind of organizing one must do in typical bureaucratic settings, in neighborhood politics, in managing the lives of one's children in a school system, and so forth. Coordination on a spot for meeting is, in principle, quite generalizable, but in actual practice it is likely to be of use in relatively restricted contexts. Incidental investment in developing one kind of network capital may have much larger payoffs in the longer run than does investment in the other kind.

Investment in network capital through participation in socially directed organizations – that is, organizations with relatively social or collective purposes, such as some of those Putnam (1995a, 1995b, 2000) discusses – may be displaced by the relatively more deliberate investment in networking for personal advantage. Indeed, those with political careers in view might participate in socially directed organizations *in order* personally to benefit from the network ties and reputational advantages they gain from such activity. (As a standard quip has it, you go to Harvard or Oxford not for the education but for the connections you make.) In the end, therefore, there might be no overall decline in network capital as Putnam supposes there is, but there might be decline in some forms of such capital when people choose to change and to invest in other forms. This may follow simply because people's goals have shifted. It would be wrong therefore to conclude prima facie that the decline of network capital in socially directed organizations *leads* to changes in goals.

Note that there are two quite different values that can come from organizational and network capital. First, the organizations and networks can be directly enabling. That is to say, they can be the vehicles we use to accomplish various purposes. For example, I may use my network to get my son's school to respond better to him. Second, they can be an arena in which we develop particular forms of human capital. That is, they can teach us how to do certain things that might be more generally valuable to us outside the context in which we learn them. For example, I may learn how to run a meeting or how to organize a group of people to take action at the Parent Teachers Association (PTA) and then I might use those skills in many other contexts. It makes good sense to reserve the terms organizational and network capital for the first of these, for the organizations and networks as vehicles for accomplishing our purposes. In a sense, the organizations and the networks just are instances of social capital. The second value, the development of individual capacities, is clearly important, but it is a matter of human capital as traditionally discussed (Schultz 1963; Becker [1964] 1975).

The question for network and organizational capital is how they benefit us. Do they benefit us by what they can do, that is, what the network or organization can do? Or do they benefit us by what they enable us to do through the particular forms of human capital that we develop in particular networks or organizations? If there is a decline in the social capital represented by such groups as the PTA or bowling leagues, the results might be both to reduce human capital for managing other people in spontaneous contexts and also to reduce the availability of actual organizations and networks to help us accomplish various things.

Fukuyama (1995) argues that participation in such networks and organizations prepares us psychologically for the demands of working in modern firms. Hence, he supposes social groups are good for the economy indirectly through the human capital that they produce. Let us try to unpack this idea. The argument is that spontaneous sociability leads us to join various social organizations, and then participation in these prepares us psychologically for working in large firms. This argument might seem to apply to a developing nation or to a subpopulation, such as various immigrant groups or ghetto poor, who have not been incorporated into the economy. But how are these groups different from the new labor forces that staffed the industrial revolution? The nascent industries of that era in Europe and North America evidently created their own human capital. It seems unlikely that much of the relevant human capital was created in spontaneous social organizations of the time. Once underway, the developing economies of many nations in our time also generate the human capital they require.

Perhaps the kinds of human capital needed today are different and are likely to be produced in social organizations such as local political groups and sports clubs. Or, more plausibly, some variant of Fukuyama's argument would apply to the kind of human capital or psychology that is needed for successful entrepreneurial activity. Such activity is needed in the drive to develop various economies as market economies and the drive to convert many centrally run economies to market economies. Market economies need capitalists, and becoming a capitalist might require the development of special forms of human capital that are related or that include some of the human capital that one would develop in the activities of spontaneous social groups.

In sum, development through participation in social organizations does not seem likely to be central to economic concerns in most of the advanced democracies, in which capitalist enterprises are alive and well and in which the generation of the relevant human capital is handled within university and other business schools, in experience on the job, and, probably, within entrepreneurial families, whose offspring tend to be much more entrepreneurial than the average person. The entrepreneurs who have made the largest difference to the exploding computer and information industries have included teenagers such as Steve Jobs and Bill Gates.

So what is to be said of the somewhat anomalous case of North America, where the social capital implicit in spontaneous social group organization has reputedly been in sharp decline for about three decades? If this decline is problematic, that could be because we will simply have fewer such organizations to use for political and other ends, or because such organizations will produce less of the human capital that might be needed in the polity and the economy. These two effects may not both be important. Indeed, one of the plausible explanations for the decline of voluntary groups is that dual career marriages reduce available time for participation in such groups. But dual careers might give both partners many opportunities to learn how to manage people, even how to organize them for action. Hence, the decline in opportunities for developing such human capital through participation in voluntary social groups might be offset – even more than offset – by opportunities to learn such things in professional life. If so, then the main loss in declining organizational capital is from the loss of the availability to us of social organizations to be used for our wider purposes, political and otherwise.[20]

In sum, we want to know two quite different things about the apparent decline in organizational capital in North America. Does it disable us politically that we have less access to voluntary and social organizations that we might be able to use to further our political goals? And are we individually disabled by our declining incidence of participation in such organizations? Interestingly, for the first question, there seem to be two quite different issues at stake in the two quite different kinds of organizations in which participation seems to be in decline. Voluntary *political organizations*, such as neighborhood action groups, seem likely to be much more readily useful in helping us achieve political goals than are *social organizations* such as choral groups and bowling leagues. Yet, the data on the declines in these two broad classes of groups seem to be quite similar (Putnam 2000). The explanation for their decline therefore evidently has much less to do with their purposes than with the characteristics of participation in them, as is suggested by many of the proposed explanations for their decline. We are not dropping out of specifically political organizations but out of voluntary organizations in general.

In what follows I wish (1) to highlight several conceptual issues that tend to get in the way of coherent argument, and (2) to focus attention on causal issues. I will organize discussion around the conceptual issues first in several sections below. Causal issues come up throughout these discussions, and I will turn to them most specifically in the section on "Trust and interpersonal capital" and in concluding remarks on the larger programs of all these scholars.

Interests, Consumptions, Welfare

We speak, sometimes almost interchangeably, of interests, consumptions, and welfare. But these are conceptually quite different. Our interests are to be in a position to consume, and consumption typically brings welfare. I have an interest in amassing resources, but resources are of no value per se – I want them only in order to be able to consume. Obviously, interests and consumptions trade off with each other. If I consume some things, I must expend some of my resources. Some social theorists argue that we should ground our normative theories in resources rather than in welfare, that certain conceptual problems in welfare make it finally an unworkable normative principle (Sen 1982: 353–69; Dworkin 2000, chs 1 and 2). Without resolving that issue, we may all readily grant that resources are means without intrinsic value and that what gives them instrumental value is the welfare they can bring us.

Having resources is in our interest because they can be used to enable consumptions, which produce or have utility. Interests are therefore merely proxy for the utility of eventual consumptions. Interests are a useful proxy for alternative consumptions just because they constitute a far less varied category than do consumptions and because they are fungible across many possible consumptions (Hardin 1988: 200). For example, resources can stand proxy for consumptions when we speak of the interests of various groups that want higher income or profit. But the costs of consumptions need not be linearly related to their utility or the enjoyment of them, because price and benefit are not at all equivalent for any particular consumption and because there may be complementarities and substitutabilities among consumptions.

Using interests as a proxy for consumptions is therefore potentially misleading, although it might often be relatively sensible. The cardinal value theory of John von Neumann (Neumann and Morgenstern [1944] 1953: Appendix) and Thomas Bayes might apply to simply conceived interests but not so readily to a panoply of consumptions with their complementarities and substitutabilities. To put this the other way around, focusing on interests allows us, perhaps wrongly, to think cardinally; focusing on consumptions virtually forces us to think ordinally.

If we include all consumptions now and into the future in our choice function, as in Kenneth Arrow's ([1951] 1963) fully determined states of affairs, interests drop out (see further, Hardin 1987). Note that interests and consumptions trade off against each other. It is against your interest to consume an opera tonight because it uses up resources – in the best seats, roughly enough to feed a family in Kenya for a year. But if you could not do such things, you would have less reason for living. It is the very point of our interest in various resources that they enable us to consume various things, and the point of consuming them is that consumption brings benefits or welfare. The Japanese novelist Yasunari Kawabata (1974: 49) elegantly frames the relation between interests and consumptions: "When one spends money, one remembers spending it even after it's gone. But when one loses the money one has saved, the very thought of saving is a bitter memory."

Capital

We may distinguish several forms of capital, including financial, physical, human, interpersonal, and Gary Becker's (1996) social and personal capital. All of these contribute to our welfare because they enable us to purchase or produce goods for consumption or to turn those goods into welfare for ourselves and others. In traditional accounts, there were only financial capital and physical capital. Theodore Schultz (1963) and Becker ([1964] 1975) are the main early developers of the analysis of human capital, which is principally education and training that enable us to produce, as physical capital in machines enables us to produce. Financial capital enables us to purchase other kinds of capital, to invest in other ways, or to purchase consumption goods directly. Physical and human capital have the quality that they do not convert into goods for consumption but that they enable us to produce goods for consumption, in a sense, far more cheaply. Hence, for example, with a relevant machine and training I can produce far more of some good in any given period of time than I could without the machine or the training. An instructive way to put this claim is that such capital is often superadditive with other inputs, such as effort.[21]

Note that money is often different from other forms of capital such as physical and human capital and, unless it is used to purchase those forms of capital, it typically does not have the multiplier or productive effects of those other forms. It is also different in that it is typically more fungible than, say, material capital in machinery, or human, social, or personal capital. Physical, human, social, and personal capital all have potential multiplier effects. Human capital differs from social and personal capital in a significant way. Human capital, such as education and training, is itself useful directly in the production of goods. Social and personal capital come in later at the point of converting the consumption of goods into welfare. Financial capital is embodied in money and other financial instruments, physical capital typically in machinery or fixed property, and human capital in educated abilities, talents, and knowledge. Again, in Coleman's phrasing, social capital is "embodied in the *relations* among persons" (Coleman 1991: 304). Indeed, he suggests it is dependent on iterated interactions, even perhaps iterated prisoner's dilemma or exchange interactions (1991: 743).

These differences can be summarized by instantiating them. The (alas, paltry) bit of money in my pocket is an instance of financial capital. The computer on which I write this is obviously an instance of physical capital. The years I spent in education and the evenings I spent in the

Becker–Coleman seminar at the University of Chicago contributed to my human capital (although they also provided
many moments of immediate pleasure). My ongoing relations
with colleagues and many others ground instances of interpersonal capital – or social capital in the sense of Coleman,
Putnam, and others. Taken together, most instances of such
capital benefit me through the consumptions they enable me
to enjoy, through the things they help me accomplish. All of
these effects on consumption and its enjoyment not only
interact with each other causally, but they also sometimes
interact through my welfare and at cost to my interests. For
example, I may indirectly gain great benefit from writing
something (I must publish or perish) while also gaining great
pleasure from it directly. Hence, keeping the separate categories of capital or the categories of capital, welfare, consumptions, and interests completely separated analytically is
often difficult or impossible.

On an expansive reading of Coleman's general statement characterizing social capital (quoted above), a well-
functioning family structure, a system of norms to regulate
cooperation and social interactions to the benefit of typical
individuals, a working legal system for enforcing contracts,
and a working language might all seem to be instances of
social capital. In his actual discussions of instances of social
capital, however, only the first two of these come up. Similarly in the work of the political scientists on social capital,
the focus is on interpersonal considerations grounded in
informal networks of interaction. Hence, these scholars evidently do not count the more substantial institutional structures of government and large organizations as instances of
their version of social capital, although these structures may
contribute to its creation in other contexts. And the mastery
of a native language may or may not be an instance of social
capital for them, whereas having English rather than, say,
Navaho as a native language is enormously more enabling
for many purposes – although Navaho was extremely valuable for secret communication by American troops during
World War II.

Yet, institutions and language enable us in many ways. For
example, the legal institutions that stand behind contracting
enable us to enter into exchanges that would be prohibitively

risky without legal enforcement of relevant obligations. We may call this *institutional capital*. It is very different from financial, physical, and human capital in that it does not directly produce goods or benefits. But it is like these insofar as it indirectly enables us to produce through protecting us against intrusions into our efforts and it provides infrastructures that make production more efficient. It is sometimes more nearly like social and personal capital in that it enables us to make the most of whatever goods we do produce and consume. But it also differs from human, social, and personal capital in that it is largely outside us. The theorists of relational law and the new institutional economists might claim that the institutional capital in the legal system is far less than we might have thought, because very much of what makes, say, contracts work is interpersonal capital.

The institutional capital in the government and legal system of the United States is enormously enabling to me. As far as I am concerned, however, it is essentially a matter of external luck that that government exists and governs over my territory. I may contribute slightly to the continued existence and power of that government and to its specific workings in particular contexts, much as I might contribute to the improvement of a machine I use in production. And, of course, it would be hard finally to abstract that government from the inputs and supports of 300 million Americans. But the contribution of any one of us is too slight to make the government seem modally to be anything other than external to us.

In sum, various forms of capital, ranging from financial to social and personal capital, cross the distinctions of interests, consumptions, and welfare. Financial capital constitutes mere resources or interests. Physical and human capital produce or enhance the production of resources and consumptions. Interpersonal and institutional capital enable us more readily to produce consumptions.

Trust and Interpersonal Capital

Institutional capital suggests the concern of the ancient Greek "Anonymous Iamblichi" (1995: 294), according to which:

"The first result of lawfulness is trust, which greatly benefits all people and is among the greatest goods. The result of trust is that property has common benefits, so that even just a little property suffices, since it is circulated, whereas without this even a great amount does not suffice." The context of the remark is a list of the benefits of lawfulness. Law (or government) enables people to trust each other enough to risk exchanges with each other, to their great benefit. The anonymous Greek author shared the central vision of Thomas Hobbes ([1651] 1994), for whom stable government was necessary in order to enable us to profit from our own efforts by protecting us from the depredations of others and to enforce our contractual relations. Trust arises in many contexts in which we both benefit from a relationship. Our interests are unlikely to be perfectly aligned, however, and a role of institutions is to block some conflicts of interest that might otherwise wreck our trust.

For Putnam and others, it is interpersonal relationships of trust that enable us to trust government, which enables government to work. Or, perhaps we can only say that for them the problematic concern is with the seeming correlation between levels of interpersonal trust and levels of trust in government – and possibly levels of performance of government. This correlation is problematic because it may suggest declining performance in the United States and some other western nations and obstacles to performance in many developing nations (but see Hardin 1999a). What is wanted is still an explanatory account of why these correlations appear to be what survey research suggests they are (for graphic representation of the correlations in the United States, see Putnam 1995a, 2000, ch. 8).

A central issue for understanding levels of trust in various societies is to grasp whether trust follows from interpersonal capital of other kinds or whether it is itself a major category of interpersonal capital. Fukuyama, Putnam, and many others seem to see it as a major category of interpersonal capital. There is likely some conceptual confusion in their claims, because the actual interpersonal capital, if there is any with respect to trust, is *those things that enable people rightly to trust, not the trust itself.* That we perhaps successfully teach our children to be trustworthy, that we design institutions to give added incentive to be trustworthy, and that we have ongoing networks of relationships with others give us grounds to trust people in many contexts. The ongoing networks are part of our interpersonal capital.

We might also suppose that the learned capacity to judge trustworthiness, both in judging specific other individuals and in judging the context in which we are dealing with them, constitutes a form of interpersonal capital. That capacity can vary substantially across individuals and may depend heavily on early upbringing (see the learning model of Hardin 1992, 2002b, ch. 5; also see Yamagishi, Kikuchi, and Kosugi 1999). Hence, families and societies that give infants and children a sense of the trustworthiness of others may thereby create substantial interpersonal capital that enables their children later to enter into cooperative arrangements relatively optimistically.

In an ongoing (roughly iterated) exchange relationship I may be able to trust you with respect to some matter in the sense that I can expect it to be your interest to take my interest in your fulfilling the trust into account. As discussed in chapter 2, there are three standard and many idiosyncratic conceptions of trust, but this one – trust as encapsulated in the interest the trusted has to fulfill the trust – gives rich explanations of many phenomena of apparent trusting and trustworthiness. In particular, it compellingly fits the pattern of most of those whom we trust, who are those with whom we are in especially rich ongoing interactions of essentially iterated exchange. If, as in this model, trust is grounded in a rich ongoing relationship, the trusted has substantial incentive to be trustworthy in order to maintain the relationship.[22] But then it is not trust but rather the ongoing relationship that constitutes our interpersonal capital. That relationship enables trust by encouraging trustworthiness, and it therefore allows us to trust and to be trusted. It is important, of course, for us to be able to be trusted, because then we can enter into cooperative arrangements with others.

A commonplace claim is that trust does not fit the encapsulated interest model because trust is inherently normative. So what of trust as a norm? There clearly cannot be a sensible norm merely to trust, because far too many people would be utterly untrustworthy in various contexts in which entrusting certain things to them would cause harm to the truster or others. There might be a norm to be trustworthy. If so, then cooperative endeavors would prosper more readily because trustworthiness would beget trust. This follows because *your being trustworthy gives us incentive to trust you* in some context in which doing so would lead to cooperation that would be beneficial to us.[23] Hence, trustworthiness might be part of interpersonal capital. It is part of that capital *not so much to the trustworthy person as to others*, who are enabled by it. Trust that is relatively blind, rather than grounded in the incentives of an ongoing relationship or in the normative trustworthiness of another, would enable others also. But it would enable them to take one-sided advantage of the gullibly trusting. Hence, trust is either a conceptual proxy for trustworthiness in the claims of Putnam and others, or it does not belong in interpersonal capital (see further, Hardin 1996).

This conclusion draws the supposedly normative sting of their analyses in part, because it could hardly come as news that trustworthiness is a good thing. They should therefore be concerned to assess declining trustworthiness rather than its resultant declining trust. Moreover, on the encapsulated interest vision of trust, their interpersonal capital is predominantly to be seen as grounded in the rationality of maintaining a cooperative stance in ongoing relationships. This, of course, recommends the use of institutional capital as well as, to a likely limited extent, norms to secure cooperation at the interpersonal level.

Blocking Social Capital

Many governments and many other institutional managers have attempted to block the development of or to break and suppress the use of social capital of various kinds. But social capital is a means, not an end, and the ends for which it can be used can be highly mutable. Block its use in one arena and it might still be used in others. For example, in 1989 the Chinese government went after the use of social capital for democratization by simply suppressing the Democracy Movement. That movement was a manifestation of growing social capital, and it presumably also contributed to the further development of such capital as well as human capital for organizational skills. The Chinese autocrats seem implicitly to recognize that social capital is a means, including a means to potentially very important things that the regime wants, especially economic development. Hence, after the Democracy Movement was squashed, the vast mobilization of educated younger people continued, but it was turned toward economic entrepreneurship at a spectacular level.

Arabic states under various socially and economically incompetent dictators have gone after the social capital itself. The difference is striking. The Arab response has typically been the exercise of a dead hand on all activity, with the result that some of the potentially wealthiest nations of the world have suffered from near stasis economically while much of the rest of the world has developed more or less steadily – and in many cases in great spurts that have transformed societies such as those of Japan, Korea, and Taiwan in the past, and are now transforming much of Central Europe, China, India, and elsewhere after the lifting of the dead hand of central control of their economies.

Many of the Arab leaders gained power through intrigues and plots that taught the wrong lesson: allowing people to organize is dangerous to the regime. Those leaders have practiced an internal version of the English system of divide and rule in India under the Raj, with its use of Muslims from one part of the subcontinent to rule over Hindu areas in other parts, and vice versa. For example, consider the tactics of Qaddafi, who early in his rule of Libya "developed a pattern of constantly transferring military and government officials from post to post and endlessly redrawing administrative boundaries – inflicting a certain chaos on the country but also insuring that no one had the means to build a power base that might challenge his" (Anderson 2003: 32). Effectively this device blocks the development of network and organizational capital – social capital – that might have been useful for positive purposes of many kinds, as well as for organizing opposition to Qaddafi's regime. The price of blocking opposition is blocking development.

The Arab states are a modern variant of many traditional forms of predatory government. The classical Chinese, Ottoman, and many other imperial rulers used their power to extract the resources on which to maintain their power and their own levels of lavish consumption. Many of the Arab leaders have not needed to extract resources from their own people – for example through taxes or taking part of the agricultural produce of their subjects – because they could simply claim state ownership of oil fields. The result is that various Qaddafis have had the resources to maintain a military grip on their populations and, in a few cases, have used some of the oil revenues to educate and house their people. The Saudi regime has used a distressing fraction of its oil wealth to maintain a disgracefully large number of boors in the lives of princes who have no social function other than to consume the society's wealth in their own entertainment. An apparent benefit of this policy for the rulers is that these potential inside contenders for rule are made relatively incompetent even to organize. Their focus on individual consumption and their lack of any organizational or functional roles keep them away from developing their own social capital for political leadership. An Ottoman ruler might have had his sons strangled. Saudi rulers let their countless sons and nephews strangle their own lives.

The devices of Qaddafi and the Saudi rulers are extremely costly to the economies of their nations. The central move in blocking or destroying social capital is to take people out of various networks in which they have ways of connecting to others to accomplish various goals. It is just the obverse of what it takes to build social capital, although building it can and commonly does happen spontaneously, without any deliberate effort.

US prisons are organized in ways that hinder the development of networks within the prisoner population, evidently just in order to maintain control over the prisoners while they are incarcerated. The long-run effect of this policy is to block the development of social and human capital that might be useful after prison. Hence, the form of incarceration reduces the chances former convicts have to succeed once they are free (Hardin 1995: 103, 106–7; Lin 2000). It reduces their development of human and social capital and it induces distrust in general.

Recall Karl Marx's ([1852] 1963; cf. Hardin 1995: 39–42) comparative analysis of the lives of peasants and factory workers in the nascent factories in France in the mid-nineteenth century (discussed in chapter 1). This analysis is one of the first articulate understandings of both the role of social capital and the failure of developing useful social capital. In Marx's account, social capital that was developed in factories not only enabled actions in the interests of workers but it also gave them daily opportunity to debate with each other and to come to understand those interests. The anomic lack of organization of peasants blocked any chance that they might develop the social capital for political mobilization in their own interests.

In many cases, social capital that essentially blocks change suggests the relevance and even desirability of Joseph Schumpeter's ([1942] 1950) creative destruction. It is only by wrecking peasant subsistence farming and many other economic forms of organization that an economy can progress to more desirable states. Although Schumpeter does not emphasize the point, destroying institutions and various economic organizations entails destroying careers and radically changing lives. Schumpeter's analysis is essentially an account of blocking social capital and the barriers it can impose.

Concluding Remarks

All of the forms of capital discussed here can interact with each other, either causally or functionally or both. The institutional capital represented by the American or British government is enormous in its impact on the lives and welfare of their citizens and on other lives as well. Indeed, a large part of the difference between, say, Russian and western economic and social life turns on differences in the quality of the respective nations' institutional capital. The interpersonal capital that contributes to successful collective endeavors at lower levels might, through these lower-level activities and perhaps directly, also be enormous in its impact on the workings of the western governments. The program of the political scientists writing on trust and social capital is to work out this particular causal role. Certain forms of interpersonal capital enable individuals to perform their tasks within institutions better than they could do otherwise and, hence, contribute to those institutions and the institutional capital that they represent.

Coleman is right that interpersonal capital is important for facilitating lower-level interactions. Oliver Williamson (1975, 1981) is right that institutional harnessing of interpersonal capital to work around hierarchical and legal constraints can be an efficient improvement on the formal hierarchy. The relational lawyers are likely right that interpersonal capital often does much of the work of facilitating contracts (Macneil 1980; Macauley 1963; also see Williamson 1985). Because it can make particular firms more efficient and can help to overcome the inefficiencies of legal devices, Fukuyama (1995) is likely right that interpersonal capital positively can affect overall economic success. It would also be right, therefore, to suppose that interpersonal capital is important in making specific government agencies work more efficiently and effectively because of the way such capital is harnessed *within* the agencies.

But is it right that widespread interpersonal capital is important for making democracy work? That it is important in this way is in essence the claim of Putnam and many others. While Coleman's argument seemingly works for the other cases of facilitating cooperation – firm success, governmental agency success, and economic performance – there is as yet no argument that unpacks, in this microlevel way, the relationships between interpersonal capital in the populace at large and the general performance and responsiveness of democratic government. Perhaps getting the arguments and the causal relations clearer will lead to insights into what the microlevel relationships are.

Suppose interpersonal capital does affect institutional success in the general way that many suppose. Then there may be substantial feedback between it and institutional capital, which enhances the prospects of interpersonal cooperation. If so, then we might expect both political and economic development to have self-reinforcing qualities that, once started, allow them to take off suddenly. This would follow already from the arguments of Williamson, the relational lawyers, and Fukuyama. And it would be reinforced still further if the arguments manqué of Putnam and others could be put into compelling form. If declining confidence in government in the United States is partly the result of a decline in social capital, the central part of the notion at issue is participation in various public-spirited and social-group organizations. Such participation seems to be in decline in the United States (Putnam 2000; but see Ladd 1996) and some, but not all, other advanced democracies (Pharr and Putnam 2000).

This seems roughly to be the story of the beginnings of the new regime of the United States under its constitution of 1788. James Madison's design of institutions under that constitution and Alexander Hamilton's monetary policies as Secretary of the Treasury through the early years of the new government were the crucial moves in building institutions that could underwrite individual confidence in dealings with others across a very broad range of actors. Any given individual must have had many trustworthy partners for various undertakings, but the institutional devices of Madison and Hamilton greatly expanded the range of people with whom the typical individual engaged in the economy could deal. That those institutions were so beneficial may then have encouraged support for them in the early years when they must have been weak and potentially unstable.

Note that all of these forms of capital are commonly invoked as enabling. Often, however, they are also constraining. As Becker (1996: 22) says, past "experiences, and the attitudes and behavior of others, frequently place more far-reaching constraints on choices than do mistakes and distortions in cognitive perceptions."[24] They do so by contributing social capital that can detract from the benefits of various consumptions. Interpersonal and institutional capital can similarly get in our way. Widespread customs and even very local practices of personal networks can impose destructive norms on people, norms that have all of the structural qualities of interpersonal capital. Institutional capital can also wreak its destructive hold, as in the eastern nations that are now trying to build new economies and political systems while partially still in the grip of old institutions.

Hence, in general, social capital has no normative valence, as suggested by the discussion of blocking social capital. It is generally about means for doing things, and the things can be hideously bad as well as good, although the literature on social capital focuses almost exclusively on the good things it can enable and it often lauds social capital as itself a wonderful thing to develop (against this tendency, see Portes and Landolt 1996). Members of such groups as the Nazi party and the Ku Klux Klan have substantial social capital that enables them to accomplish the grim results they produce. One is reminded of the obstinate focus on the good aspects of community in the massive communitarian literature, in which it is virtually seen as offensive to note that community can be exclusionary and vicious, both to outsiders and to insiders (such as the women of many fundamentalist groups). Community and social capital are not per se good. It is a grand normative fiction of our time to suppose that they are.

5
Trust on the Internet

Let us extend the discussion of social capital to a potentially very important new form: the internet. The internet is arguably the most remarkable addition to social capital in our time, and its workings are only beginning to be discovered and understood. The vast outpouring of work on it is bound to continue and to open up new ideas about social interaction, especially social interaction in this peculiar form. Discussion therefore cannot be definitive and is probably bound to be fairly speculative. For example, some argue that, although there are similarities, groups on the internet are distinctively different from groups in the "real world" (McKenna and Green 2002). Others argue that, although there are differences, the two kinds of group are distinctively similar and should be treated as such (Komito 1998).

For our purposes, the internet poses a peculiarly extreme context for developing trust. It almost meets the conditions of experimental games in which you might know virtually nothing about another with whom you are interacting. All that you know might be the immediate record of the other's behavior in your interaction. There might be no reputational effects, only iteration effects. Hence, the internet has some but not all of the liabilities of contemporary research on experimental games. The most important difference in some (but not all) contexts is that we can establish ongoing relationships over the internet, carefully choosing to interact with the same people repeatedly (Coye and Cook 2004; Kollock 1999; Matzat 2004). Although there can be complications of free-riding and confusion of the identities of the participants, groups or dyads can commonly achieve the iterated interactions that enable them to give incentives to participants to live up to their reputations and to use future interactions as incentives to be cooperative in the present, momentary interaction. For example, auction sites, such as eBay, can differentiate frequent repeat sellers – called power sellers – from occasional sellers. Hence power sellers can establish reputations that give them substantial advantages (Snijders and Zijdeman 2004).

Moreover, the scale of potential benefits and costs is probably relatively evident in many internet exchanges, and there are usually severe constraints on these. Hence, the internet does not have the liabilities for researching trust that contemporary survey research has with its blandly open-ended questions. Doing research on the extent and possibilities of trust in internet relationships does, however, have the liability that the internet is relatively new and that research paradigms for it are still in an early developmental stage.

As a form of social capital the internet is not reducible in its characteristics to other forms of social capital, such as ordinary networks of people who more or less know each other, organizations whose connections and talents may be tapped by "users," and so forth. The social capital of the internet – which we may call internet capital to distinguish it from network and organizational capital – is huge. It enables us to do many things with radically greater efficiency than we could do them without the internet as an enabler. Because the internet itself is enormous, with hundreds of millions of participants in it, a typical individual's contribution to its capital is negligible, although some individuals make major contributions, as the inventors of Google and the creators of several reference works have done. Many other kinds of network are far smaller with far fewer participants. In these, an individual's contribution can proportionately be relatively large, so that your using the network might increase its value to all other users in the same context.

For all its magic, however, the internet has what seem to be major drawbacks that make it not merely a high-speed analog of traditional devices. It can do some things better but other things much less well than traditional devices can. At both extremes, the differences are so great as to be not merely quantitative but also qualitative. The things it can do better are often things that can readily be checked and verified. The things that it often cannot do include securing commitments for action, either for spontaneous or highly organized cooperation.

In general, on the internet trust as encapsulated interest is likely to work best if we have an offline relationship that gives us each a greater stake in our relationship as well as more knowledge about each other than we could typically get from merely an internet relationship – without a nagging worry whether all that knowledge is true. Our problem here, therefore, is to determine how we can come to be confident of our internet relationships. We also face that problem for our dealings with many, perhaps most people offline. We can canvass the devices that help us offline to see whether they could also work online. Many of them cannot, because our relationships on the internet are too focused and not thick enough.

One of the devices we have to secure trustworthy behavior from those on whom we have to rely, even though we would not trust them in any strong sense, is to have third-party certification of some kind. This can range from the advice of a trusted neighbor who says that a plumber is reliable, to the backing of a professional or institutional body that tests or has opportunity to evaluate competence. It could also include cases in which the third party more or less guarantees the performance of someone we are in no position to trust but with whom we would like to be able to cooperate on something. Such third-party devices for the internet are only in development, but finding ways to make trustworthiness detectable may offer some agency opportunity to establish a profitable role in rating internet traders and perhaps other kinds of users as well (Güth and Kliemt 2004). For example, in response to a disturbingly high level of fraud, eBay requires that sellers of travel vouchers must be registered with an independent verification company (Hafner 2004). The growth of such rating agencies in traditional markets for loans, jobs, services, and other beneficial exchanges has been a very important part of developing the modern market economy. Their role is essentially to establish credentials for trustworthy dealing, just as professional associations and credit bureaus have done historically for contexts in which, virtually in principle, we could not judge certain providers independently on our own (see Cook, Hardin, and Levi 2005, ch. 5). Our inability on our own to judge providers of various services over the internet is not dramatically different from our inability to judge the quality of a doctor or a lawyer whose services we need.

Trust arises where there is some, perhaps substantial, risk of default or untrustworthy behavior. If there were no risk that another would default, it would be virtually pointless to speak of trust. Hence, we have a real stake in the judgment of any trusting relationship. With no risk, we might wrongly suppose we come to know someone well enough to judge how they will behave. But if we have faced someone repeatedly in contexts in which we are both at risk, we can finally know with great confidence whether the other is reliable and, even more important, we can judge whether the other has an interest in maintaining our relationship and therefore has not only the competence but also the will to fulfill our trust. In very anomic contexts, we cannot typically have either kind of information about those with whom we interact: neither the very general knowledge of their competence nor the personally very specific knowledge of their interest in fulfilling our trust.

Internet Commerce

What are the risks that we take over the internet that we can successfully handle so that our "partners" on the web do not take unreasonable advantage of us? For commercial dealings, we do take some risks, although we substantially reduce these in the same way we do in commercial dealings off the web. We rely on dealers' reputations. Recall from chapter 2 that this is not a backward-looking estimate of their character, but a forward-looking claim about their interests. For example, a store's reputation is more important by far to the store than it is to you. Therefore the store cultivates a good reputation, which it can do by performing well in its dealings with customers. The dealers from whom we wish to buy are those who care about their *future* reputation and who therefore have an interest in dealing equitably with us as a way of investing in their future reputation and thereby securing future business.

This is the nature of John Mueller's account of the early history of Wanamaker's department store in Philadelphia. John Wanamaker supposed that he could attract far more customers if he could convince people that his policy was not caveat emptor – let the buyer beware – which was the policy of virtually all sellers in his time. He therefore advertised that his store would take back anything it sold for a full refund, no questions asked (Mueller 1999: 79–80). When I deal with Amazon.com, I think of it no differently than I think of a major department store on Lexington Avenue in New York. *It is a business that needs repeat customers.* And its success suggests that it has figured out how to keep its customers coming back for more.

In this respect, power sellers on internet auction sites and the internet stores have incentives very much like those of standard retailers. In both cases it should be clear to the sellers that their future opportunities to sell more depend on their living up to their past reputations. Repeat sellers on the internet have much of the incentive structure of an ordinary retail store. Their reliability brings them further business. A signal difference in many cases is that potential buyers over the internet, especially from the auction sites, cannot first check out the specific piece of merchandise they wish to buy, as they can do in traditional stores. An occasional individual seller on an internet auction site is in a position analogous to that of an individual seller of a used car. The odds that the used car seller has gone into the market rather than trading the car through a dealer. suggests that the car might not pass muster with a dealer. Hence, the used car market tends to be a market for lemons (Akerlof 1970). If it is the first time you go onto the internet to sell, say, your antique lamp, you can probably expect the bids to be low because the bidders will discount the value of your lamp. This is little different from what happens when you advertise your car in the local want-ads. Buyers will possibly discount your lamp even more than a buyer would discount a used car, however, because there are substantial opportunities for (and a high incidence of) fraud on internet auction markets.

Ebay therefore has had a "vice president for rules, trust, and safety" (Hafner 2004) – presumably such an officer is not required by ordinary retail dealers. The internet has unique capacity to organize an auction at a global level, but it has little capacity to police it. An ordinary auction house is highly localized, but it has many devices to prevent abuse and fraud upfront. Ironically, while it is surely harder to shoplift from a store over the internet than from a store on the avenue, it is apparently easier to commit theft and fraud on an internet auction site than in an auction house.

Note that in our commercial dealings with stores, trust is not generally an issue. Competence is virtually the whole story. We want them to be competent in serving their customers well. We want them to be competent in understanding that their future reputation is important to them and in understanding that they want repeat customers, not one-time customers whom they could readily cheat without concern for the future. Shopping from a standard retailer over the internet does not add any significant complication over the normal nature of our offline dealings with retail stores. In the eBay auction system, which enables people to do something that would be far less efficient if restricted to face-to-face markets, fraud and bad form have room to play. It is in such contexts and certain other areas where trust is absent that various devices for ensuring reliable behavior become important. As discussed below, the chief other major category of such problems so far encountered might be in the use of the internet for email for various purposes.

The most obvious feature of the internet for this discussion is that it is a vast collection of networks. Offline networks commonly enable us to build up trust relationships. Often these are very limited and focused. Let us therefore specifically address the possibilities for network trust offline before going back to trust on the internet.

Trustworthiness in Communities and Networks

In small, close communities cooperation can be managed by the rule of norms that are backed by spontaneous sanctions from the members of the community itself. Hence, those members are essentially trustworthy in their dealings with each other. Even today, many of us live at least parts of our lives in small "communities" in which norms govern much of our behavior toward each other. But large parts of our lives are not regulated by close communal ties and the spontaneous sanctions to which they give rise. We live in more nearly urban contexts in which we interact with large numbers of people, many of whom we may never expect to see again after a single interaction. More significantly, we have ongoing relationships with extensive networks of people. We secure what we need through multiple networks, some of them overlapping in part but some of them essentially separate from others (see further, Cook and Hardin 2001; see also Fischer 1982, Watters 2003). In these contexts, we commonly develop trust relationships in the sense of trust as encapsulated interests. We reciprocate favors over many years with people whom we grow to trust because we value our relationships with them and we suppose they value their relationships with us.

Although there are exceptions, most of our relationships over the internet cannot have the quality of small, close communities that are spontaneously regulated by norms. But they also cannot usually fit the structure of trust relations, because such relations are typically embedded in networks or are built up in dyadic relationships that go on for a long time. It is difficult to imagine devices that would work for trust on the internet with people who do not have further interactions with each other off the internet, interactions in which trust could be grounded. The best we can do in many cases is to establish ongoing relationships (Coye and Cook 2004). We can have smallish networks that have more or less stable memberships and that are involved in frequent interactions on the internet. But the trust relations that normally grow in iterated and network interactions offline grow out of interactions in which there is something at stake, often something very significant at stake. I do things for you and you do things for me and we trust each other with respect to some range of things.

On the internet, when there is something of significant value at stake, the potential partners to an exchange might not know each other from before and might typically not expect ever to encounter each other again. Only an ongoing, stable institution, such as Amazon.com or the website of a traditional retailer, can expect to be judged by its reputation because only such an entity can have enough interactions with others to be able to establish a reputation. Such an entity does not need to trust its customers, who can obtain goods or services only by first paying for them. Indeed, internet retailers do not even suffer the steady losses of shoplifting that afflict ordinary stores.

Enabling Cooperation

In our kind of society, we have cooperative relations within dyads of close friends or relatives; within subcommunities that are small and close enough to be regulated by norms; in exchange relations in varied networks that are regulated by the force of the iterated exchange incentive and its proxy in reputation; and in institutionally protected exchanges. It is only in the first and third of these – dyadic exchange relations and cooperative relationships organized within networks that are typically restricted to specific issues – that trust as encapsulated interest is fundamentally important. For the small community devices of norms and sanctions to work, relationships must be relatively thick. Network exchange relations commonly involve relatively thin relationships that are focused on narrow issues, such as doing reciprocal favors over some range of issues. Dyadic relations can range from the narrowly focused to the nearly all-encompassing, as in a good marriage (Franz Kafka might add: if there has ever been a good marriage).[25]

The use of norms grounded in communal sanctions will commonly not work for so decentralized and vast a system as the internet. A principal reason for this is that the users of the internet are not also involved with each other in manifold other venues or in overlapping networks, and they do not need to be. You may not even know who are the other person or people with whom you deal; and the other or others may evaporate into the ether at any moment. Potential endgame effects are apt to loom much larger in internet than in real-world interactions. Endgame effects of instant withdrawal are likely to be relatively rare in small community relations and even in friendship relationships, although there can be sudden blow-ups that lead to complete breaks even in such relationships. You may be involved offline with many of those with whom you deal over the internet, but not with most of the people who might use the internet to abuse your interests in some way. For the former, the norms that govern our interactions will often typically precede the internet in our relationship or will have transcended our relationship over the net.

The internet is the most extreme version yet established of an exceedingly large anomic society. In its Greek origins, anomic means lawless; in contemporary English it more often means normlessness. Much of our use of the internet is normless. Moreover, almost all of it is lawless. One can commit fraud over the internet, and that would be subject to legal action. But many people spend more than a thousand hours a year on the internet and are never involved in anything that would rise to the level of legal scrutiny – unless they happen to download copyrighted music or videos. In its normlessness and anonymity, the internet has some of the characteristics of urban life during those periods when one is anonymously walking the streets and meeting no one whom one knows. But it goes far beyond such anomic interactions in that it often actually involves exchanges and even some degree of dependence on one another. Very little, if any, of our standard vocabulary for describing and explaining human relationships fits many of our relationships on the internet.

Nevertheless, the internet is enormously valuable to us. It enables us to do many things that would otherwise be extremely difficult or even nearly impossible. In my milieu, for example, I can use the internet to find out things that it would take days to discover through traditional means, such as library researches. It provides – or is – a novel form of social capital. Often when I am seeking a fact on the internet, the sources on which I stumble turn out to be the same sources I would have consulted in traditional searches. Sometimes, however, they turn out to be the websites of industrious hobbyists whose catalogs of facts and stories are a labor of love. Once I do find out something, however, I can then very efficiently double-check it in traditional ways or by consulting traditional sources – such as newspapers and encyclopedias – over the web. Apart from its email function and its capacity to deliver documents instantly, the internet for me is primarily a device for discovery of facts, but I am not finally dependent on it for verification of facts.[26]

Politics on the Internet

Many political activists and various political theorists have speculated or even hoped to see the internet spark new levels of active participation in politics. The greatest achievement to date in the use of the internet in politics was the 2004 campaign for president of the US by Howard Dean. Dean raised surprisingly large sums through internet solicitations and organized meetings across the nation by coordinating over the internet. More than 60 percent of the money he raised came from donors who contributed $200 or less, while all other candidates got the bulk of their receipts from donors who contributed $2,000 (the legal limit for an individual contribution). Moreover, Dean's contributors generally found their way to giving by themselves, not through the prodding of a friend or other associate, which is the way most political money is raised.

A striking feature of internet politicking so far is that it seems to depersonalize participation. Individuals are not brought into a campaign by networks to which they belong. Rather, they merely show up at internet coordinated events and they write (usually small) checks. Matthew Hindman (2004: 126) notes that in "the civic voluntarism model, ground-level social networks should have been necessary to attract and retain supporters. In Dean's case, these networks were largely absent [and the] new technology allowed Dean to create local, decentralized social networks from scratch." This runs oddly contrary to the idea of participatory democracy, which many people expected the web to foster. In the vision of participatory democrats, we the citizens join together in various groups to push our causes. Those groups were expected to be formed by personal relationships. Instead, in Dean's campaign, they were individuals acting spontaneously on their own to seek out the campaign's events.

The internet is like other forms of social capital in that its valence is neutral. It can be used to accomplish harmful things and beneficial things. It can be used to bring families and friends closer together and it can be used to enable terrorists to coordinate massive destruction. It may even be unusual on this score because it may have harmful effects merely from the way it works in some arenas. Many of those who comment on its effects in politics note that it tends to lead participants to read only the materials of their favorite candidates and entirely to ignore competing views, from which they might gain valuable insights. It is not even the undecided but only the already committed who seek out information on candidates' websites (Bimber and Davis 2003, ch. 4; Hindman 2004: 124). They apparently seek affirmation more than information. At best, this means that perhaps they are more strongly mobilized on behalf of their views after finding such complete affirmation of them. It does not mean that they are particularly articulate in defending their views against alternatives that they prefer to ignore almost entirely anyway.

In fairness, however, it is not only the internet that causes such narrowing of views. The world of books can play a similarly narrowing role. Amazon.com and Barnes&Noble.com list the books that "customers who bought this book also bought." Valdis Krebs used these data to construct two nearly exclusive networks of books. One collection is liberal books – which are apparently read only by liberals. The other collection is conservative books, which are apparently read (or at least bought) only by conservatives (*New York Times*, Mar. 13, 2004, pp. B7 and B9).[27] (Krebs notes that there are far fewer books in the conservative network.) The internet must merely heighten this already pronounced effect of separating these two groups into networks between which there is essentially no conversation. Indeed, political campaigns before the internet were similarly almost entirely a matter of preaching to the converted (Bimber and Davis 2003).

What the Web Enables Us to Be

One of the peculiarities of the life of the internet is discussed very entertainingly by Sherry Turkle. Turkle says of herself that, on the internet, she is a "multiple, distributed system." She is a clinical psychologist, social scientist, author, professor, and cyberspace explorer, where she travels under many identities or names. She could do far more, as many of those she has studied do, and travel under essentially untraceable names that could let her act out any persona she chooses over the anonymous internet. We cannot do that as readily, if at all, in real life.[28] Therefore her title, "Who Am We?" She supposes, however, in the contemporary postmodern vision that we are, in some meaningful sense, all of these identities, that we are multiple in nature (Turkle 1996).

Turkle has been characterized as the anthropologist or ethnographer of the internet, although it might be more accurate to see her as a psychologist of the internet. She argues that "computers are not just changing our lives but changing ourselves" (Turkle 1996). In a sense, she is generally interested in answering the question what – or who – the internet enables us to be. She focuses on what the internet does *to* us. I am more generally interested here in what the internet enables us to do. I want to understand what it can do *for* us. This focus pushes us to study the internet as a form of social capital. We can invest in that capital, as millions of people and institutions are doing, thereby increasing the value of the internet to others, and we can put it to use, as even more millions are doing.

A striking case of intensive activity on the internet is by those who play internet games, which are games that are on the web and that players can enter into or exit from more or less at will. Players can number into the millions and can come from anywhere on the globe (Turkle 1996). They are typically anonymous to each other, although each can have a name for purposes of the game so that players know with "whom" they are playing in the limited sense of knowing whether any player was in the game before. Such internet game players do not need trust or any normative constraint, such as reciprocity or fairness, to be able to play in orderly ways. Their moves are constrained by the computer program. Their interactions do not have the free form of ordinary life, although a freer form can presumably be increasingly programmed into such games. The players form a network that is both gigantic in the number of agents in the network and tiny in the form of what the network manages for them. Some of them might spend 40 hours a week in the game, so that it is quantitatively a large part of their lives. It might also take on a large psychological role for them. But it remains highly focused and unlike the melee of ordinary life. It finally bears little resemblance to what we call networks in our lives offline.

Turkle has interviewed many players of such online games to determine what the playing, usually anonymously, does for them when there are well over a million regular participants from many societies over a long period of time. Those facts alone make it sound like an important social phenomenon that we might want to understand. If we are to determine the larger social effects and significance of this phenomenon, we need to know who are the people and what are their larger roles in the society. Or in Turkle's language we need to know more about the people that they are outside their personas as players in the game.

Those who are interested in the phenomenon of television in contemporary lives do studies of such things. Television watching similarly occupies a large part of many lives, upwards of 40 hours each week. (That is hard to imagine, because it is equivalent to *six hours every day*, say from 6.00 until midnight every evening.) For some of these people television is not a substitute for life in other forms but is merely an entertainment during lives that would otherwise be even more empty and lonely. For many, however, it is thought to be a major alternative to living in supposedly more interesting ways. Robert Putnam thinks that the distractions of television have substantially reduced the social capital that comes from participation in various social groups and organizations (Putnam 1995a, 2000).

Eventually, we should want to have similar accounts of the effects of living life on the internet. Presumably, internet gaming does some of what television does to social participation. Quite possibly, however, this claim is wrong, because the gamers might be people who are only loosely connected to the kinds of groups and organizations that interest Putnam and other critics of television. Maybe, in Putnam's metaphor, they would be bowling alone with or without the internet, and many of them may be especially attracted to the internet in large part because it allows them to bowl alone and anonymously. Perhaps they would not be more socially active even if the internet collapsed. Of course, it could be the case that computer usage from an early age has created part of the personalities of those who are now turned off of standard categories of social participation. What we need, if we are to understand such worries and loose claims, are hard studies that go beyond anecdotal stories of particular individuals, as interesting and suggestive as these are.

Internet Pneumatique

Among the most striking aspects of the internet is the ease with which one can write letters and thereby maintain relationships across massive distances and long times. I am involved with a fairly large number of email correspondents, but for us the internet is merely a convenience. It is true that the convenience may be so dramatic that it changes our relationships, much the way the relationships of Parisians in the time of Marcel Proust or of Czechs in Prague in the time of Franz Kafka must have been changed by the fact that they could exchange several letters in a single day by use of the pneumatique. Such quick exchange may tend to heat up the contents of the exchanges and therefore the relationships themselves.

The ease and alacrity of email also change the scale of our correspondence. I receive and write upwards of a dozen real letters a day in exchanges with real associates, and in addition I get nudged several times daily (these do not count as real letters). Before email, I wrote and received far fewer letters. And I relatively seldom received letters from people I did not know. After being out of the country for more than a week some time ago, I returned to find more than three hundred real messages (after deleting the roughly equal number of junk emails). I did not quickly make it through that backlog and some of it may have died of neglect. There are probably people in the world who are offended at my inattention. Yet I spend more than an hour daily doing email – there were few days before email when I spent so much time on such correspondence.

For Turkle, internet romance via email is a major topic. For many of us, presumably it is not a major part of our lives, but for some it apparently is. It is possible that the distancing of the internet is actually an enabler for initiating romantic attachments because one can come to know a lot about another person's sense of humor, intellect, and character more generally in a remarkably safe venue in which it is relatively easy just to drop the correspondence and the correspondent at will.[29] If the relationship seems appealing, it can always be transferred to the real world. I am told by someone whose authority is probably great that email romancers know that they should attempt a meeting soon – before they develop a strong attachment to someone they would never have liked in person. Without such a meeting, they are at risk of falling in love with an ethereal persona, who is not a person, but eventually suffering the anguish of a broken romance with a real person. Email, weirdly, has returned us to the era of the troubadours, with their fancifully embellished beloveds admired from a great distance.

This is a context in which a person might have something at risk so that there is at least a possibility that trust would arise. The risk is that, in order to pursue the relationship further, one must eventually reveal one's identity. Indeed, such revelation is likely to be an element in demonstrating one's trustworthiness and, therefore, in establishing a trust relationship. For many of us, especially in our lives in business, the professions, and academia, we are more or less fully exposed in many ways on the web. We have websites that include lots of information, some of which could readily be linked to other sources to fill in many gaps. One could say – in the vacuous vernacular – that one trusts everyone else with all of this information. It would be far more meaningful to say that one thinks it worth the risk to put out so much information, because, for example, it enables one to make connections that would be valuable. For academics, easing the way for others to read our work is likely to be beneficial to us. There may be heightened risks (for example, of plagiarism or vicious criticism) from such easy exposure, but they seem likely to be outweighed by the benefits.

Even while we are exposed in such hopefully constructive ways, we can also lead relatively secret lives on the web by the use of other email names through anonymous providers. To do so is somewhat cumbersome for those who are not very heavily invested in browsing and using the web, because it means checking mail on different systems. For those who are a bit klutzy, this sets up opportunities for embarrassment when using the wrong address fully identifies the writer or chat room visitor.

There is an apparently complex and specific aspect of the regime of email that has not been adequately addressed. Within organizations, people often develop paranoid cognitions and engage in dysphoric ruminations about their colleagues. A reason for this is that often they have too little information about what the colleagues actually think, and psychologically they tend to assume that no information is bad information (Kramer 1994, 1998). What seems like ordinary paranoia is often justified, especially in contexts in which there is a clear or potential conflict of interest or a power differential (Cook, Hardin, and Levi 2005, ch. 3). Paranoid cognition is perhaps especially prevalent in international relations, especially in contexts in which there is a serious risk of conflict and even hostility. International relations are therefore perhaps thought to be far more hostile than they are in objective fact.

Paranoid cognition is not itself justified by objective grounds for fearing another, but if there is any reason for concern, that concern is apt to be heightened by communications that are very terse, as email communications commonly are. The medium seems to encourage efficient brevity,[30] and there is not enough time for extensive responses to all our emails. There is not much to read between the lines when there are only one or two lines. The medium typically lacks the expansive graciousness of much of traditional letter writing. It also lacks visual clues to what the correspondent might mean, in particular it misses cues that suggest that the correspondent is smiling rather than scowling – although there are many cues that are conveyable over the internet (Coye and Cook 2004: 229). Of course, it also lacks the tones of voice that suggest the mood of a person over the telephone. The use of cryptic funny faces as punctuation marks must often help, as though the writer were saying, "Don't take that seriously." Unfortunately, such faces have become too common to be very revealing and there are seldom scowling faces to give us an accurate measure of real variation in mood. Having no baseline, we evidently sometimes invent one.

Insofar as paranoid cognition and dysphoric rumination are in substantial part responses to the terse quality of email and its common lack of tacitly informative cues, the internet may often actually foster distrust even when there is no objective reason for it and may exacerbate it when there is at least some reason for it. There is nothing additionally at stake in email correspondence beyond what would be at stake in traditional forms of communication, and yet the form may cause us to respond and act as though there is. A major part of that form is its instantaneity.

Concluding Remarks

What makes for trust in ordinary contexts is the richness of our iterated interactions. The richness makes the relationships more valuable so that we want to maintain them; and this is our evidence of each other's trustworthiness. Internet relationships typically are very narrowly focused on what would be merely a limited piece of an ordinary relationship. In this respect, internet relationships are more nearly like commonplace commercial relationships, in that they are often not repeated but are one-shot. For commercial dealings, however, we have the devices of the market for establishing and correcting reputations that give us and our commercial partners incentives to behave well. It is that broader set of relationships that secures our commercial dealings. If we have a richer relationship with someone with whom we have internet dealings, that richness most likely comes from our further interactions offline. There may be a few internet relationships that become moderately rich, as long-standing self-help groups reputedly do. But the bulk of our internet dealings that are not merely extensions of offline relationships are too focused and pared down for them to rise to the level of grounding trustworthiness and securing trust.

We could conclude that we need devices for securing reliable interactions on the internet. Or we could conclude contrariwise that the internet is inherently not very useful for handling the kinds of problem that dyadic trust as encapsulated interest, small-community norms, offline network connections, and third-party enforcers handle in the offline world. So far, it appears that the latter conclusion is correct. Indeed, it is probably wrong even to speak of trust in this context because it is straightforwardly the interest of, for example, internet retailers to be reliable. Even those who insist on speaking of trust in these contexts still recognize that trade needs a feedback mechanism to regulate behavior (Bolton, Katok, and Ockenfels 2004). That is to say, it must be made the interest of traders to be reliable, as in the arguments of Mueller on the origins of honest practices in large retail stores. The one area in which trust seems to be at issue on the internet is in ordinary communication via email. But this is an arena in which most of our dealings are with people with whom we have extensive offline dealings. The ease of using email might facilitate the strengthening of our trust relationships with those *with whom we are already connected* and with those who come to us with third-party commendation. It might also facilitate the quick breakdown of a relationship if paranoid cognition comes into play.

The case for and against the importance – or even the relevance or possibility – of trust on the internet is still open for most contexts. At the moment, what we need if a positive case is to be made is explanations of how trust can arise, be strengthened, and be tested on the internet. That would include an account of just what kinds of risk we face on the internet when it enables others to work against our interests. For many of us, trust is beside the point in any case, except perhaps in our email exchanges or self-help groups, because the internet is merely a form of social capital that we can put to use with sometimes extraordinary results – and sometimes great frustration. It is merely the analog of a very large, extremely well organized library whose content can be scanned almost instantly, coupled with an even higher speed and internationalized pneumatique.

In this the internet is like other categories of social capital. It is also like them in that to use it well requires substantial human capital. I have two research assistants who virtually waltz through the internet with dazzling ease and grace. It is human capital such as theirs and of the programmers of various search engines, such as Google, that makes the social capital of the internet enormously valuable.

It has been suggested that, in a way similar to what happens in internet politicking, the internet might balkanize science by simplifying the narrowing of focus of scientists onto things immediately related to their own work, so that there will be less cross-fertilization (Alstyne and Brynjolsson 1996). This could happen because scientists' networks might be narrowly focused on the large number of people around the world who do what they do, because it is now easy to focus this way by using the internet to seek out specifically relevant works. Unfortunately, while seeking out similar specialists across the globe, scientists might have fewer interactions with those who are geographically nearer but intellectually less related. Oddly, the political and the scientific results of narrowed focus that worry some observers are closely analogous. One might imagine that, in the world of published science, as in the world of ideologically focused books, there are similarly disjoint networks with little cross talk.

Although it may sound perverse to put it this way, the central issue in making the web be more richly useful to us, beyond its being a quick research and communication tool, is how to create networks on the internet that approach the richness of the networks most of us have in our offline lives. So far, the internet, the biggest network of all history, may have relatively little of the often rich and manifold value of usual networks. Those who have hoped the internet might enhance participatory democracy and civic life more generally might be disappointed in its performance so far, although the case of Howard Dean's campaign for the presidency in 2004 suggests great promise. Many of us may be happy enough with its powers of research and communication. It is not only a new form of social capital, it is also a new form of network. It is at once extraordinarily extensive and remarkably shallow in its reach.

At the nearly opposite extreme from the internet games played simultaneously by countless people are self-help groups in which a few people may regularly bare their personal problems for each other to discuss. Typically, the members of such groups go by names that do not reveal their actual identities. Indeed, in some cases members of such groups have been discovered to be dishonest in pretending to be like the members of the group when they are quite different. While such a group works, however, the members may develop trust relations. They are constantly at risk of being attacked and sometimes even of being exposed, especially if there are internet savvy members of the group who can ferret out the real world identities of participants.

So what of trust on the internet? For most of our dealings on the internet, trust is not an issue virtually by definition because we face no risk of any significance and we do not deal in relational interactions over many rounds. There is no place for trust to take hold. In many other dealings, the biggest risk is violation of our privacy, for example, as the result of uncontrollable wider publication of an embarrassing email or, as in the self-help group, the discovery of our actual identity.

6
Terrorism and Distrust

Terrorism raises two important issues in trust. First, obviously, is the problem of how terrorists can cooperate in extraordinary actions that put themselves at great risk, including risk of betrayal. Second is the problem of how a society – even one with standard liberal protections of civil liberties – can avoid pervasive distrust of subcommunities, domestic and foreign, from which terrorists might come. The two problems interact in that the devices for securing cooperative commitments among potential terrorists run counter to the plausible visions of society that include strong protections of civil liberties. In these visions, civil liberties are needed to protect individuals from abuse by the state at various levels of government. It is the state through its justice system, not through protections of civil liberties, that must protect individuals against each other.

Part of the source of popular fear of Islamist fanatics is that they isolate themselves in exclusionary communities where we cannot know them and, perhaps more importantly, they cannot know us. In such communities they can sustain beliefs that would seem lunatic for anyone in the larger society (Hardin 2001). It would be of great interest to know how many of the recent terrorists became committed to violence after they moved to the West, where some of them were, for example, seemingly normal students in Hamburg and southern California. They apparently did not go west in order to be terrorists, but were brought to their communal, exclusionary epistemology when they were members of small immigrant groups sequestered in a larger society. Their isolation coupled with suspicions about their actual beliefs and motivations may provoke a form of generalized distrust of everyone from their general background, the vast majority of whom are very unlikely to become terrorists. Let us call this group-generalized distrust.

Efforts to prevent terrorist attacks are not like efforts to control ordinary crime and they may undercut the regime of civil liberties that depends on the assumption that miscreants actually have interests – largely material – that are shared by the larger society. Pervasive distrust of a potentially terrorist group may seemingly give the state license to take extraordinarily illiberal actions. Such actions might be well received by the majority of citizens who do not think their own liberties are at risk from actions against members of identifiable groups from which terrorists are most likely to come. Against this relatively smug stance, however, one might note that the extremist militia groups in the US claim to be defending their own civil liberties. Given the government's disastrously violent attack on the radical Branch Davidian community in Waco, Texas, on April 19, 1993, we cannot easily say they are wrong (see Boyer 1995).

The focus in this discussion is on groups as well as individuals, with groups and their members commonly the objects of trust or distrust and with individuals in the large society trusting or distrusting them. If one were to do survey research on the distribution of distrust of groups, one would wish to have responses to questions about members of identifiable groups as well as responses to questions about various groups as groups. For example, a woman might generally react differently toward women and toward men on many ordinary issues having nothing to do with gender per se (Cook, Hardin, and Levi 2005, ch. 2). If she is an American citizen and she meets two anonymous strangers, one of whom has certain identifying characteristics of an American and the other of whom has foreign characteristics, she might deal with them very differently. In particular, she might more readily take the risk of relying on the first and be somewhat more wary of relying on the second for some minor matter.

If the other person has a heavy accent and Middle Eastern facial features, she might be only slightly more wary of that person than of the first person in dealing with some minor matter of the moment. But she might be extremely wary of the *group* from which the second person comes. She might therefore even want quite different policies for dealing with the different groups from which these two "anonymous" strangers come. We know from varied contexts that people can have a more positive view of individuals from a group than they have of the group. Many Americans, for example, very nearly revile government bureaucrats as a class even though they often think well of all of the bureaucrats with whom they have had any dealings (Klein 1994). There must be many Americans who have trusted Arab-American associates but who generally distrust Arabs as a group.

The Epistemology of Close Communities

Norms of communal cooperation, as discussed in chapter 1, are effective only to the extent that members want to continue as members. In this respect, such norms, although vague in their range, are similar to trust as encapsulated interest (as spelled out in chapter 2). Such trust generally depends on the trustworthiness induced by the desire to maintain the relationship. Network organization of cooperation can be governed by overlapping dyadic encapsulated-interest trust relationships and by reputational effects that are a proxy for such trust relationships. Hence, such trust relations are a substitute for traditional communal norms for contexts in which the norms would no longer work because the web of dense interactions that both defines and enforces the norms is absent. When cooperation is organized by communal norms, it can become highly exclusionary, so that only members of the community can have cooperative relations with those in the community. In such a case, the norms of cooperativeness are norms of exclusion (Hardin 1995, ch. 4).

For many fundamentalist groups, continued loyalty to the group and its beliefs is secured by isolating the group and its members from many other influences so that relations within the community are governed by extensive norms of exclusion. When this happens, it is not only trust relations but also basic beliefs that are constrained. If we encounter no one with contrary beliefs, our own beliefs will tend to prevail by inertia and lack of questioning and they will be reinforced by our secluded, exclusionary community. There are many strong, extreme beliefs about religious issues as well as about many other things. Many of these views have to be wrong for the simple reasons that they differ from each other and that each denies the truth of the others. The two matters for which such staunch loyalty to unquestioned beliefs are politically most important are probably religious and nationalist commitments (see further, Hardin 1997, 2001). Such beliefs are often maintained by blocking our alternative views and by sanctioning those within the group who stray.

Consider a very peaceful group, the devoutly religious Amish who live mostly in the Midwest of the United States and into Canada. The Amish are not hostile to others but merely want to continue in their own ways (this is evidently true at least for older adults) and they are very nearly apolitical. The Old Order Amish of Wisconsin have long striven to protect their children against corrupting their beliefs by taking them out of school at age 14. Wisconsin law requires education through age 16 and Wisconsin officials attempted to force the Amish children to continue in school by fining parents who took their children out of school early. (The fines were not large.) Amish leaders won the legal right to stop education at age 14 in a famous Supreme Court case of 1972: *Wisconsin v. Yoder et al.* The Amish and the Supreme Court opinion both argue that further education was likely to corrupt Amish children's beliefs. They therefore concluded that the constitutional separation of church and state meant that Amish parents could not be forced to expose their children's beliefs to such severe tests (see further, Hardin 1995: 201–3).

It is widely supposed that such narrow views cannot readily be sustained by many people if they are constantly exposed to very different views. Often the reason people alter their views about ordinary matters is that they experience things that run counter to the beliefs, or they deal with people who question their beliefs. Indeed, this was the forcefully articulated view of Amish leaders in Wisconsin. They very well understood that keeping their children away from the broader American culture was virtually necessary to keep them locked in the faith.

Extremist and fundamentalist groups are often able to block such corrective devices as come from interactions in the larger society. Some of the terrorism on the ground in the Middle East seems to fit easily with the usual view that isolation is important in strengthening and sustaining extremist beliefs. Terrorist training often takes place in very isolated camps, such as those of al-Qaeda, where there is no contrary view and where every individual is constantly reinforced in the group's belief system. There might be very few broader social influences that are discussed or that can survive in the face of constant hortatory indoctrination along with fairly substantial deprivation of kinds of social interaction that most people enjoy (see, for example, Crossette 2001).

All of this works because most of what anyone knows comes from hearsay, from "experts" such as a neighborhood gossip, a newspaper, or, in exceptional cases, an encyclopedia or other authoritative source. What isolation from other influences does is give us a crippled epistemology (Hardin 2001). We are unable to come to know many things and we have no reason to reconsider the things we think we know.

On this account, maintenance of extremist beliefs depends on embedding the believers in a closed community. It needn't be entirely closed, just mostly. For example, an Amish farmer might know several non-Amish with whom he deals commercially. But he doesn't immerse himself in their communal life and he knows little of it. Members of the extremist militias of Idaho, Michigan, Montana, and Wyoming are very isolated from other influences. Their friends are other militia members. The Unabomber led the life of a nearly complete loner – he evidently had no further influences on his beliefs beyond the things he chose to read. But he was a loner in the further sense that he was not part of a larger, more threatening movement of terrorists who might wreak far greater harm than any ordinarily equipped loner.

Our embeddedness in an exclusive community can both enable and constrain us. It enables us to rely on fellow group members in ways and to a degree that it would be implausible for us to rely on people in the larger society outside our community. There is a bit of truth in the chief normative claim of communitarianism, which is that community can be very supportive to us and make daily life more congenial and comfortable and is therefore in some sense good for us. It offers us the epistemological comforts of home (see further, Hardin 1995: 54, 77, 89, 90). Another bit of truth in communitarianism, which, however, has negative implications, is that community can suppress us and keep us in line in ways that make little sense except that they are the ways of the community. Communities can destroy individuals and their lives. Communitarian philosophers in our time see the good side of community as overwhelmingly, even definitively, good and they are virtually blind to the potentially harmful side of it (see further, Hardin 1995, ch. 7). Unfortunately, however, there is a brutal and unavoidable conflict inherent in the idea of exclusionary communities in which adults secure their own values by constraining their children's future lives.

Narrowing one's associations to others in an isolated extremist group cripples one's epistemology by blocking out general questioning of the group's beliefs (Hardin 2001). To an outsider those beliefs might be utterly crazy. Indeed, virtually all strong religious beliefs sound crazy or silly to those who do not share them. Social scientists and historians might explain the prevalence of certain religious beliefs, but their explanations are likely to render the content of the beliefs contingent on historical accidents rather than on theological truths.

Generalized Trust, Generalized Distrust

There is a fairly extensive literature on so-called generalized trust, which is trust in the anonymous or general other person, including strangers, whom we might encounter, perhaps with some restrictions on what issues would come under that trust.[31] Evidence for such generalized trust comes primarily from three standard survey questions in the General Social Survey (see chapter 3). In answering these questions, people commonly say that most people can be trusted or, on a multilevel scale, they choose a relatively high level of confidence in others' trustworthiness. It is all too easy to read such responses very loosely. If I say I can trust most people most of the time, I may merely be saying I trust most of *those I do actually deal with* most of the time. Of course, that is partly why I deal with them and not lots of other people whom I would not trust most of the time (I might actively distrust some of them and be agnostic about others).

In principle, however, the idea of generalized trust has two odd features. First, it sounds more nearly like an account of simple *expectations* than an account of trust. In this account, I supposedly think *everyone* is reliable up to some degree independently of who they are or what relationship I have with them. I think this of them the way I might think the typical person would behave in certain ways in various contexts. This sounds more like optimism about the cooperativeness of my fellows than trust in them. Moreover, at best, such optimism is likely to be about specific kinds of people, so that it depends on stereotyping.

Second, when survey respondents say they trust most people most of the time, this is, as discussed in chapter 3, an elliptical claim. They do not mean that, if a random stranger on the street were to ask for a loan of, say, a hundred dollars, they would trust that person to repay and would therefore make the loan. This open-ended answer to a badly framed, vague question is just a loose way of saying they would trust most people within somewhat narrow limits. Moreover, it is also elliptical in its reference to "most people." Few of the respondents would genuinely trust just anyone much at all.

The survey results cannot be read to show that there is genuinely generalized trust. The respondents are forced by the vagueness of the questions to give vague answers and it is a misdescription to label their responses as generalized trust. Note, incidentally, that for Rotter's interpersonal trust scale there is no room for a category of generalized trust even in his psychological view that some people are inherently more trusting than others. That his scale divides into three independent factors suggests, indeed, that degrees of trust must vary according to the stereotypical character of the potential objects of trust, whether they are, for example, parents, politicians, or strangers (Wright and Tedeschi 1975). It would not be hard to frame survey questions that would allow us to multiply these categories and to find fine distinctions in whom people do or would say they do trust.

At best, in any case, what is called generalized trust must be merely a matter of relatively positive expectations of the trustworthiness, cooperativeness, or helpfulness of others. It is the stance of, for example, the child who has grown up in a benign environment in which virtually everyone has always been trustworthy. That former child now faces others with relatively positive expectations by inductive generalization (see further, Hardin 2002b, ch. 5). The value of quasi-generalized trust is the value of such an upbringing: it gives us the sense of running little risk in cooperating with others, so that we may more readily enter into relationships with them. Of course, such generalized optimism is a value only if others are relatively likely to be trustworthy.

Why does anyone speak of generalized trust? It is an implausible notion. In any real-world context, I trust some more than others and I trust any given person more about some things than about others and more in some contexts than in others. I may be more optimistic in my expectations of others' trustworthiness on first encounters than you are, but apart from such a general fact I do not have generalized trust. I might also typecast many people and suppose some of the types are likely to be trustworthy enough to justify the risk of cooperating with them, other types less so, and still others not at all. However, this is far short of generalized trust. It is merely optimism about certain others. Such optimism from typecasting makes rational sense, just as typecasting of those whom one might employ makes rational sense as a first, crude indicator of competence or commitment. This is the rationale in Gary Becker's (1971) analysis of discrimination in hiring.

Many, maybe even most, claims for generalized trust can readily be restated as claims that, in contexts in which trust generally pays off, it makes sense to risk entering into exchanges even with those whom one cannot claim to trust in the encapsulated interest sense – because one does not yet have an ongoing relationship with them and nor does one have reasons of reputation to trust them. This is not a claim that one trusts those others, but only that one has relatively

optimistic expectations of being able to build successful relationships with certain, perhaps numerous, others (although
surely not with just anyone). Hence generalized trust seems
likely to be nothing more than an optimistic assessment of
trustworthiness and willingness therefore to take small risks
on dealing with others whom one does not yet know. That
assessment would be corrected if the optimism proved to be
unwarranted because people and agencies in the relevant
context proved not to be generally trustworthy.

Whereas generalized trust or group-generalized trust
makes little or no sense (other than as a claim of optimism),
group-generalized distrust in many contexts makes very good
sense. If you were Jewish, Gypsy, or gay, you had good reason
to distrust all officers of the Nazi state and probably most
citizens in Nazi Germany as well. American Indians of the
western plains had very good reason to distrust whites.
During Milosevic's wars and pogroms, Serbs, Croatians, and
Muslims in then Yugoslavia had increasingly good reasons to
distrust most members of the other groups, especially while
the latter were acting as groups. Blacks in the United States
have long had very good reason to distrust white police
officers, not only in the south but in many northern cities as
well. In all of these cases, distrust is defined by the belief
that members of the other groups and their representatives
are hostile to one's interests. Trust relationships between
members of these various groups are the unusual cases that
require explanation; the relatively group-generalized distrust
is easy to understand and justify. In all of these particular
cases, the proportion of those from another group who were
not to be trusted was generally quite large – or, in the
Yugoslav case, it became quite large very quickly after various
atrocities and brutalities.

Consider just one of these archetypical cases. In the
American south during the days of Jim Crow segregation
laws and practices, white police forces and courts intimidated
and harassed blacks. Ordinary white citizens often were also
abusive and scornful to blacks. But frequent lynchings must
have had an especially detrimental effect on race relations and
on the prospects for interracial trust. From 1883 to 1960, the
awful era of lynching in the United States, an estimated 4,742
people were openly and publicly killed by lynch mobs. The

large majority were blacks, often for no crime. The number of blacks lynched as a form of racist terror is probably more than the number of people killed in all the terrorist attacks on Israel in the recent Intifadas or in the attacks of September 11 in the United States. A recent book displays photographs of uncounted whites – numbering into the thousands at single events – celebrating or merely spectating at these lynchings (Allen et al. 2000; also see Dray 2002). Some of the photographs derive from postcards that were made and sold at the events and then mailed to others. One of these postcards pictures a crowd around the charred remains of Jesse Washington, who was lynched in Waco, Texas, in 1916. The postcard is inscribed: "This is the barbecue we had last night my picture is to the left with a cross over it your son Joe" (Allen et al. 2000, plate 26; see further, McMurtry 2000: 28). In the face of such events, generalized distrust of whites by blacks must have been pervasive and perhaps still is.

In the current circumstances of mostly Arab and Islamic terrorism against Israel and the West and much of the rest of the world, it is surely a very tiny fraction of all Arabs and Islamists who are genuinely a threat, but the scale of their threat may make many Israelis and westerners wary of virtually all Arabs and Islamists, because what bothers them is roughly the product of the likelihood of doing harm and the scale of the harm that is likely. Moreover, many who are not prospects for taking terrorist action evidently sympathize with and even support those actions (see, for example, Addario 2001).

On the encapsulated interest theory of trust, I cannot trust the members of a circumscribed community and they cannot trust me, because we are not involved in ongoing relationships that we could sustain to our benefit. We might distrust each other, but we could not trust each other. Mere statistical doubt in the likely trustworthiness of the members of some identifiable group can be sufficient to induce distrust of all members of the group with whom one has no personal relationship on which to have established trust. Such distrust would be group-generalized distrust. This statistical doubt can trump relational considerations and can block the initial risk-taking that might allow for a test of another individual's trustworthiness by stereotyping that individual as primarily a member of some group. If there are many people with whom one can have a particular beneficial interaction, narrowing the set by excluding certain stereotypes is efficient and we commonly do such things in many contexts. Unfortunately, however, excluding very systematically on the basis of ethnicity or race becomes pervasively destructive of community relations.

Terrorist Communities

Now turn to the trust that seems to make terrorist commitment and action possible. Terrorist communities seem likely to be merely extreme cases of exclusionary groups more generally. They are, of course, special in their purposes, but they may also be special in the small size of their face-to-face communities. Terrorism that is well organized, as opposed to the anarchically, individually motivated terrorism of the Unabomber, poses a potentially grievous problem. Terrorists, almost by definition, seem to identify very strongly with a particular community and see some other community as hostile to their own community's prospects. Therefore they are likely to find it natural to live in exclusionary groups. Therefore there is likely to be little evidence of their role in the society they wish to attack.

An astonishing fact about the Unabomber is that he was evidently able to sustain his antitechnology views and his energies in sending out letter bombs while living in virtual isolation from everyone. Already, that suggests problematic sanity. The terrorists who attacked the World Trade Center and the Pentagon seemingly lived in very small communities of sometimes only two people. In some ways, the internet allows individuals and small groups to be quite isolated while nevertheless maintaining substantial contact with others of like mind. Islamic terrorists in the West can be almost completely isolated individually while maintaining nearly instant, frequent contact with each other and with groups in the Middle East, Pakistan, or Afghanistan, as well as with groups of other potential terrorists in target nations.

Immigrants who join an extant subcommunity of fellow nationals are likely to be integrated into a stable set of values and commitments and are likely to find that their interests depend in large part on building and maintaining good relations within that community. They are likely to experience an analog of what sociologists in the Marxist tradition call embourgeoisement. When workers begin to partake of the pleasures of the bourgeoisie – owning homes and cars and having their children educated – they tend to adopt bourgeois values and become conservatively concerned with maintaining and maybe advancing their status within the system (Goldthorpe et al. 1969). Then they cease to be revolutionary and, indeed, they may even cease to vote for workers' parties in democratic elections. Part of the life of the so-called "sleepers" – dedicated terrorists living in the country they plan eventually to attack in some way – is to avoid any analog of embourgeoisement by avoiding the development of significant ties to others in the society in which they await their day of violence. Rich relationships in the larger society might block the prospect of ever adopting terrorist commitments for those not already part of a terrorist group.

Civil Liberties and Potential Terrorists

In the face of threats from hostile exclusionary groups that solidify their beliefs through isolation and thereby engender potentially deep distrust, it is not psychologically reasonable to expect people actually to believe that the full program of civil liberties that protect citizens should be invoked on behalf of members of a potentially terrorist group. Because the language of such protections is overwhelmingly universalistic, many citizens quoted in the recent American press and many of those with whom I speak, especially students in my classes on law and morality, democracy, and nationalism, find themselves being inconsistent in arguing both for the maintenance of civil liberties and for the strong surveillance of Arabs in the United States and restrictions on their travel or immigration to the United States. If the vocabulary of civil liberties distinguished between citizens and noncitizens, who might be seen as in limbo while establishing the credentials for gaining citizenship, it might be easy for these same people to defend civil liberties for citizens without wavering, while demanding different treatment of noncitizens.

The painfully tainted history of race relations in the United States makes it very difficult to treat groups differently, to stereotype, in the law. The law must be universal. This history therefore probably makes it difficult even to treat noncitizens differently from citizens in many respects. Indeed, for most of a century, civil liberties law in the United States has largely been defined by the group-level conflict of racism, especially in the criminal law, in laws regulating state provisions of various benefits such as education, and in some categories of regulatory law governing travel, real estate, and other housing. There have been other issues, but year to year for many decades, much of American civil liberties law has been about protection of blacks accused of or under trial for crimes of various kinds and blacks abused by various government officials. Many of the resultant civil liberties doctrines might never have arisen except for the abuses of racism on the part of officials of various governments, local, state, and federal. The law specifically addresses race.

Legal action against ordinary miscreants has two aspects: backward looking and forward looking. It is backward looking when it punishes a particular action. It is forward looking when it deters action from even happening. Backward-looking punishment of ordinary crimes acts simultaneously to help deter future crimes. Punishment of acts of fanatical terrorism is likely to have little or no deterrent effect. The retributivist school of thought holds that criminal law should strictly be backward looking, not forward looking. Such law should not be about deterrence but about punishment of wrongdoing. This view is often associated with the view that what counts as a crime is not merely conventionally determined by what the law says but that it is a moral wrong per se and that it deserves punishment. This general view does not easily fit such problems as terrorism, especially suicidal terrorism. Punishment after the fact is often irrelevant (not always – those who planned and carried out the 1993 bombing of the World Trade Center were tried and sentenced to long jail terms, and some of the recent terrorists in Madrid and London have apparently been tracked down). Even when it is not irrelevant, our overwhelming concern is to deter terrorism. The only effective deterrence is de facto total deterrence. For example, the only ways to deter suicide bombers are to stop them in their tracks and to jail them or block their entry in advance.

The liberal state is not well designed for the latter form of deterrence. Indeed, the liberal state is not well designed for the kinds of surveillance needed for either form of deterrence. The liberal state was designed to achieve a high level of social order without massively infringing the liberties of ordinary citizens. The Nazi state, the states of many military juntas, and the states of many fundamentalist regimes, such as that in Saudi Arabia, can adopt the draconian devices that suppress such fanatical actions. While killing and suppressing those who might have been destructive if allowed to run free, they presumably make many errors of commitment – killing or otherwise suppressing the innocent. As its central purpose, a regime of civil liberties is designed to protect against such errors of commitment, which wreck the lives of the innocent. Even for the prosecution of ordinary crimes, errors of commitment are seemingly common, as is suggested by recent uses of DNA evidence to exonerate many men on death row in various states of the United States.

The idea of protecting civil liberties was to protect those for whom the social order is beneficial. People who benefit from the social order will generally not attempt to wreck it. Citizens who build their lives on the extant social order are likely to acquiesce in government actions to maintain that order. This is arguably the most that can be said for the commonplace claim that government requires trust if it is to be stable (as in Levi 1997). Citizens will be supportive of well-directed policy action and of a criminal justice system that seems to work properly. Most citizens will also acquiesce in government secrecy in certain matters, such as strategic planning during wartime and weapons designs, and in some degree of police surveillance through checking identity cards such as drivers licenses or passports.

Concluding Remarks

So who were the men and perhaps women who organized and carried out the attacks on the World Trade Center and the Pentagon in September 2001? If their narrowly focused, very extreme beliefs required sustenance from a community in which they lived and with whom they shared their beliefs, then there must be a significant number of others living in Florida, New Jersey, and maybe other places such as Minnesota and Arizona, because some of these people had evidently been in the US for many years. In the news coverage so far, people are reported to say some of them were friendly and polite. But no one says any of them was a friend. They seem to have managed to keep themselves apart.

Were they like the Unabomber – individuals living in our society but almost totally isolated, holding strong beliefs and dealing with almost no one? Or were they more nearly like the Amish – a community with close relationships and constant affirmation of and support for their beliefs? If they and others who might follow them are like the Unabomber, they will be hard to find and track. Indeed, it will be extremely difficult even to identify any of them before they act. If they are like the Amish, their communities in various target nations might be located and we might come to understand their goals.

We might suppose that they are more like the communal Amish than the isolated Unabomber. Some of them needed to use the American world of flight training to become competent to do what they did, so they had to move in and out of the larger American society and they had to be in the US for a moderately long time. Hence, they were involved in some limited networks into the larger society as necessary to sustain themselves, to learn to fly, and to use other resources to help them in planning and executing their horrendous actions. But they were evidently otherwise isolated from that society. Their isolation made them less known or even knowable. Had they had richer relationships in the larger society, they might have been identifiable, but then their motivations might also have been or become different so that there would have been nothing of special public interest to know them for.

We evidently face Hobbes's problem of groups that are misfit for society because they wish to destroy it rather than to benefit from it. But we face that problem in the era of strong protections of civil liberties and we would be aghast at Hobbes's own solution of his problem, which would be to kill or drive out committed terrorists (if we could identify them). Western liberal societies cannot adopt such a Hobbesian domestic policy without harming and maybe even wrecking themselves (although in Afghanistan and Iraq the US and UK have adopted the equivalent of a Hobbesian foreign policy). We have our commitment to civil liberties because we long ago overcame our problems of grievous social disorder and were therefore able to focus our efforts on less destructive issues than those of religious fanatics and aristocratic glory seekers. The religious fanatics among current terrorists seem fanatical at levels that the various Protestant sects of Hobbes's time could not have rivaled. Some of the current terrorists might be more nearly romantic glory seekers than religious fanatics. Indeed, Osama bin Laden has seemed in his videotapes to be playing rather than to be deeply religiously motivated, although that appearance may be little more than a trick of his personality.

Western liberal democracies overcame their own problems of disorder primarily through economic advances that led to the quasi-embourgeoisement of the large majority of all citizens. In part, it is that economic success that is now the target of terrorist actions. Because the terrorists' goal is destruction rather than something more nearly like theft, liberals have no incentive system that can overcome their urges. Treating them as criminals if they are caught in planning or carrying out attacks makes sense ex post, but the threat of such sanctions may play little or no role in motivating them ex ante. Our issue is almost entirely that ex ante problem. It is not an entirely novel problem, but it is entirely novel to face it in an advanced liberal democracy that has no theory or institutional devices for dealing with it.

It is disheartening that the contemporary problem of Islamic terrorism provokes, in a new form, the old problem of pervasive group-generalized distrust of a particular ethnically defined group within the society. More generally, the ongoing threat of massive terrorism is likely to be highly corrosive to a liberal society. When a tiny fraction of an identifiable group are likely to wreak horrendous harms, the product of the small probability and the scale of the harm leads to group-generalized distrust that seems to be statistically justified and that may lead to strong support for anti-libertarian policies that work against all the members of the group. The capacity for solidary trust within terrorist enclaves produces disproportionate distrust within the larger society.

7
Liberal Distrust

The beginning of political and economic liberalism is distrust. This claim is clearer for economic liberalism than for political liberalism because it is overtly foundational in economic liberalism, which was directed against the intrusions of the state in economic affairs. Those intrusions typically had the obvious purpose of securing economic advantages for some by restricting opportunities for others, although some of them may have been merely capricious or ignorantly intended. Hostility to such economic intrusions led to the form of the American Constitution, with its principal purpose to restrict government and its actions in the economy or, in the lexicon of the time, in commerce. James Madison saw the creation of an open economy of untrammeled commerce as the main achievement of the new constitution.

That creation was essentially dependent on the simple Commerce Clause, which blocked actions by states to interfere – for the benefit of the states, their agents, or particular interests with preferred access to political power – with interstate commerce in the United States and to control international trade (Hardin 1999c: 241–8 and passim).[32] Madison wanted to lodge commerce powers in a national government; and to block that government's abuse of its power, he wanted it to be generally weak. Indeed, the greatest strength of the national government in its beginnings was the power to reduce the power of the individual states, especially to block their intrusions into commerce. The massively powerful state we know today bears almost no resemblance to the government designed by Madison's generation, many of whom thought that their own government was already far too powerful and therefore loathsome. As with the European Union today, the overall result initially was the reduction of the economic power of government as a whole, counting both state and national governments together. Commerce was freed from both of them and the result was a more dynamic economy with much freer flow of commerce.

Why distrust? Because the experiences both of England for centuries before the US Constitution and of the 13 states during their brief union under the Articles of Confederation were rent by government actions to control the economy in often destructive ways. Often there were identifiable beneficiaries of the controls. Hence, given power to intervene, one could be fairly sure that governments would often do so. The straightforward incentives of government agents were to arrange benefits for themselves through impositions on others. Such incentives are a recipe for distrust in the sense that those on the wrong end of the interventions could see that their own interests were sacrificed for others merely because someone had the power to intervene.

Even before Madison and his arguments for the US Constitution, the recognition that governments were prone to abusing people in such ways was a central part of the development of liberal thought, especially in the work of John Locke, David Hume, and Adam Smith. The original contributions of Madison to this long tradition were, first, to create a government that was hemmed in by itself so that it could not easily overreach its authority and, second, to give that government very little authority while also diminishing the authority of the individual states.

Let us consider the liberal tradition of distrust from Locke to Madison. Until Smith, the dominant element in that tradition was political liberalism and concern with government actions against individual freedoms. In the writings of Smith and Madison the dominant element is concern with economic liberalism, perhaps in part because the prospects of political liberalism had already improved significantly in England and, after some religious excesses such as the Salem witch trials, it was perhaps about as secure in most of the American colonies as anywhere. In part, the difference in the earlier and later writings is the growing mastery of nascent economic theory that could make sense of the reasons for failure and success and that could essentially define the grounds of distrust. In part, however, the differences might have followed from the sense that economic liberty would help to secure political liberty, as Locke's defense of property already had done and as Madison's vision of a multiplicity of economic interests suggested.

From Locke to Smith

Perhaps the most provocative of all the liberal claims for distrust in government is Hume's ([1742] 1985: 42) remark that government institutions must be designed to work even if they are staffed by knaves: "Political writers have established it as a maxim, that, in contriving any system of government, and fixing the several checks and controuls of the constitution, every man ought to be supposed a knave, and to have no other end, in all his actions, than private interest." Hume actually had a better opinion of people than this injunction seems to imply to many readers. But he grasped the essential fact that it is *government's performance at the extreme* that we have to fear. Hence, we should design government to be safe against extreme performance. His claim is one of risk aversion, not of misanthropy. Hence, for Hume it is occasional agents of the government whom we must distrust. Hobbes also holds that there need be only some bad apples in a society without government for that society to descend to his awful state of nature. He further supposes, from his experience of the ugliness of the English Civil War, that such bad apples are available.

Well before Hume, however, this view of wariness toward government is already well stated by Locke ([1690] 1988, §143), who opposed lodging too much power in a single branch of government (as Hobbes wished to do) because "it may be too great a temptation to human frailty apt to grasp at power." He makes other similar remarks about the tendency of people to seek their own advantage and to use the powers of government to do so. Indeed, he supposes that "the properest way to prevent the evil, is to shew them the danger and injustice of it, who are under the greatest temptation to run into it." The people show their leaders by rebelling (§226).

Smith ([1776] 1976 (book 4, ch. 7, sec. c): 630) is more singularly focused on economic regulation and less on political liberty. He does not present a theory of liberal distrust, but his general argument is that we will all prosper best if we decide for ourselves what to do in the economy. Our pursuit of our interests will lead us into the best possible results. He rails against the abuses of mercantilism and other state controls over economic activity, such as empowering guilds of men in various professions to decide who will be allowed to work in those professions.

Both the Hobbesian and the later liberal constraints are part of a two-stage choice. We generally coordinate on creating institutions for constraining certain classes of behavior, and then the institutions implement the constraints. In *Federalist* 49, Madison notes that resort to the people should be reserved for "certain great and extraordinary occasions." Ratifying a constitution was one of those extraordinary occasions. In an extreme statement of this dual structure of choice, Madison argued that an advantage of the particular form of representative government proposed for the United States in its new constitution was "*the total exclusion of the people in their collective capacity* from any share" in the government (*Federalist* 63, para. 14, emphasis in original). Madison here refers to the role of representatives. They should actually legislate and not merely report what their constituents want. Montesquieu makes a seemingly similar claim that the people are competent to elect but not to govern (Montesquieu [1748] 1989 (book 2, ch. 2): 12). But Montesquieu holds that the people are incompetent to understand what the more qualified governors can understand. John Adams ([1787] 1987: 59) says that "the people" is an incoherent notion if "by *the people* is meant the whole body of a great nation [who] can never act, consult, or reason together."

Madison's constraint on voters is motivated by representative democratic theory rather than by a judgment of the weak character of the mass (see further, Beer 1993: 227). That is to say, popular sovereignty should stop at the adoption of the constitution. It must seem perplexing to anyone committed to unvarnished popular sovereignty that this was an argument made in public to win popular support for the constitution. But Madison's focus here is on the design of the government, and not, of course, on the adoption of policy as the result of elections that do express popular sovereignty. The very idea of creating institutions to design and implement policies inherently makes sense only if they are to act in ways that the entire populace acting together could not do, as in the two-stage theory of Hobbes. The people create a sovereign, but then the sovereign governs. The American people created institutions through the adoption of the constitution in 1788, and those institutions govern. The people participate in politics through elections and other activities, but they do not directly govern.

In addition to distrusting self-interested motivations of officials, all of these liberals also share with Hobbes some doubt in the commitment and capacity of officials to pursue the interests of the people even when not distracted by their own interests. As Hobbes ([1651] 1994 (ch. 8): 40) puts it, "A plain husbandman is more prudent in affairs of his own house than a privy councilor in the affairs of another man."

Finally, all of these liberals are more complex than merely to distrust government. They all also believe with Hobbes that government is necessary for our prosperity and even survival. Locke supposes that government is necessary for maintaining property rights. Hume and Smith assert its competence in building the infrastructures without which industry and commerce could not flourish. At the end of *Federalist 55*, Madison agrees with this hopeful view. And all of them share with Hobbes the view that government is necessary for protecting us against each other; both Locke and Hobbes suppose that only government can keep religious conflict at bay. Perhaps, again, the strongest statement is from Hume ([1739–40] 1978, 3.2.7), who argues that government, "tho' compos'd of men subject to all human infirmities, becomes, by one of the finest and most subtle inventions imaginable, a composition, which is, in some measure, exempted from all these infirmities." How is this accomplished? By having officials be constrained by institutions. This is the overwhelming response to distrust of government. It must be hemmed in by institutional devices, including institutions that contest with each other.

But, far more than was true for Hobbes, all of the other early liberals see government as a mixed blessing and they want it to stay out of some aspects of our lives.

Madison and the US Constitution

The United States was created on a principle or theory of distrust in government. There were two focuses of this distrust: individual political liberties and economic liberties. Briefly consider the concern with individual political liberties. A reading of the Bill of Rights and the Constitution suggests some of the reasons for belief in the liberal theory of distrust. In general, the long history of conflicts over which family should be the royal house in England involved constant abuses of power for the sake of gaining or maintaining power through the office of king or queen. (See Byrne (1983) for an account of the insidious conflict between Henry VIII and Lord Lisle of the formerly royal Plantagenet family.) More particularly, the experience of life in England during the struggles over the seventeenth-century Civil War and the ominous prerogatives of the king in stationing troops in homes, impressing men into the navy, subjecting potential opponents to the Star Chamber, locking people away indefinitely without charge, and other abuses or forms of cavalier disregard of individuals informs the Bill of Rights and its restrictions on government prerogative. Its rights are a litany of their time and some of them would not be issues in more recent constitutions.

The economic concern was essentially that of Adam Smith's hostility to mercantilism, which was, in England, essentially the sometimes rigid control of trade and the granting of monopolies to family favorites of the king. Of course, Smith's chief work on the subject, *The Wealth of Nations* ([1776] 1976), was available before the US Constitution but only after the Declaration of Independence. Still, many of the central ideas on economics and the criticisms of mercantilism were not strictly original with Smith and were widely in discussion.

To collapse a complex history, those who wanted to have a bill of rights included in the US constitution were evidently far more bothered by English abuses of political liberties. Madison, however, seems to have been motivated primarily by the abuses of economic freedoms in England in its mercantilist manipulations of the economy for royal benefit. For Madison, the chief reason for calling the failed Annapolis Convention in 1786 and then, in 1787, the Philadelphia Convention (now called the Constitutional Convention) was de facto to institute a stronger but still weak national government to override the state governments on issues of commerce. Its chief domestic power was to constrain the 13 states. Madison thought the state governments were irresponsible in their petty and destructive regulation of commerce. The constitution drafted in Philadelphia was designed to embody the Commerce Clause, to stop restrictions on interstate commerce through tariffs and other devices (Hardin 1999c: 241–8).

Madison seems to have distrusted government's predilection for intrusions in the economy because they were partisan (as in the granting of monopolies) and were in cavalier disregard of citizens and their interests. Smith partly dislikes mercantilism because it includes a false theory of how an economy can be developed. According to that false theory domestic producers and the national economy should benefit from restraints on trade carefully managed by the state. Smith holds that free trade is generally a more beneficial policy even though it entails foreign competition for domestic producers. He thinks such competition is generally beneficial in the incentives it gives to improve production.

One of Madison's advantages at the convention in Philadelphia was that he was not especially a partisan of some group's interest. He was interested in the general success of all commerce and of the productive classes because he recognized that economic success must be joint, and not separable. Plantation owners could prosper only if financiers, shippers, traders, and manufacturers prospered. They had complementary capacities and they would benefit mutually

from the elimination of barriers to their economic cooperation. This was in essence his clearest economic insight and it
was seemingly beyond many others at the time. Partisans are
commonly very good at pointing out what problems are in
need of investigation; but they may be nearly useless at actually investigating them. Alexander Hamilton or Thomas
Jefferson would surely have written far worse constitutions
than Madison helped to contrive. When Madison became a
political (not economic) partisan during the period of the
creation of the Jeffersonian Republican (now Democratic)
party, he often made arguments that belied his earlier claims.
Hence, had he been merely recommending reforms to an ongoing political order, we might suppose he would merely have
been a carefully partisan politician rather than the brilliant
master builder of Philadelphia.

Of course, the concern with personal political liberties was
also from experience, even if not from theory. The best theory
was roughly Hume's maxim that we should design government to work well even if staffed by knaves. This is a kind
of fail-safe theory. In Philadelphia, Madison was opposed to
including a bill of rights in the constitution. He seems to have
believed that the new government would be sufficiently weak
that it could not tread very heavily on political liberties any
more than it could on economic liberties. But even the experience of the US Constitution shows how serious the problem
of state intrusions in political freedom are. The Alien and
Sedition Acts under John Adams, the second president of
the new country, revealed that despite clear constitutional
protections, individual liberties were at risk even from a
relatively weak government.

To some extent Madison was right in supposing that
abuses of political liberties would be lessened by making government too weak to intrude in the economy. The Soviet government was designed to intrude heavily into the economy
and to design and manage a new socialist economic system.
But the power it had for that purpose enabled its government
to exert capricious control over personal liberties that had
no relation to economic success or failure. Poets, artists,
and composers were suppressed as brutally as anyone who
opposed or got in the way of Soviet economic policies (or
of Stalin's career). Hume's fail-safe rule on government is

depressingly relevant to many centralized regimes of the twentieth century, which all too often have had either knaves such as Hitler and Idi Amin, or economically ignorant and incompetent leaders such as Nehru and Muammar Qaddafi in control.

Of the men at the Philadelphia Convention, Madison was singularly the deepest thinker and the greatest architect of the new constitution. It was probably a matter of great good fortune that Thomas Jefferson was in France at the time so that Madison was essentially a free agent to do what he thought best. In Jefferson's presence, he would likely have been far less independent. Among the theorists whom the conventioneers read, the most influential was probably Montesquieu. Montesquieu was especially influential in espousing the views that animated the strongest potential opposing groups for Madison's designs to create a new national government that could dominate the state governments (which he might as soon have abolished). That opposition, which was too diverse for any single positive or defining label, has become known by the negative label, the Anti-Federalists, as though to imply that they only opposed and did not support anything. That inference is partly wrong because some among them had a theory of their own, a theory that implied a form of organization for the society.

Many of the Anti-Federalists, including many of the most articulate among them, believed that the best form of liberal government is republican government in a small society, as Montesquieu argues. Hence, they wanted essentially local government with either extremely weak national government (such as that under the then governing Articles of Confederation) or none at all. In their visions these men were forerunners of today's communitarians. Because many of them mistakenly supposed that whatever happened in Philadelphia would be subject to rejection by the congress of the Articles of Confederation (in which each single state had veto power), they were absent from the debates and the voting in Philadelphia. Madison and company well enough understood that going to the then extant congress would be death to their new designs because they could be virtually certain that Rhode Island would veto its changes (soon thereafter Rhode Island voted not to ratify the constitution and remained outside the new nation until halfway through George Washington's first term in office as president). Instead they sent their constitution to individual state conventions. In essence, their actions were a violation of the then extant law of the Articles, because the congress had authorized the Philadelphia Convention only to propose revisions to the Articles. Instead, the convention ignored the Articles and wrote a new constitution.

Madison clearly thought Montesquieu fundamentally mistaken in his central claim that only a small republic, with its homogeneity of interests and opinions, could hope to have stable government. Madison held, on the contrary, that the most grievous threat to liberty in the United States was from the state governments – especially during the preceding decade that of the smallest of the states, Rhode Island. He argued that a national government would give better protection against the tyrannies of petty, local majorities. Madison's argument in *Federalist* 10 is perhaps the strongest refutation we have of Montesquieu. (For a recent account of Madison's liberalism, see Beer (1993: 244–340). Beer attributes some of Madison's arguments to Hume ([1752] 1985) and to James Harrington (1656).) Madison therefore wanted a dominating national government – not a strong national government but strong only relative to the state governments. He wanted to break the power of the states over commerce.

Because the only way to construct a new national government was through something like the Philadelphia Convention, at which the representation was by state delegations, there was essentially no hope of eliminating the states, and much of what Madison wanted could not be achieved (as he openly explains in *Federalist* 40). Still, Madison had no vision of a government as strong as, say, that of France in the seventeenth and eighteenth centuries or of any advanced nation today. His intention seems to have been to create a government that would have *less power* overall in domestic relations than the collection of states plus the weak government of the Articles had had, while it would have *more power* in international relations, especially with respect to trade but also with respect to national defense.

Madison saw the states as arbitrary in their economic policies, which in his vocabulary is virtually the opposite of liberal. This was a problem because he thought Montesquieu was wrong in supposing that small republics would be homogeneous enough not to have conflicts, as he said in a letter of 1787 to Jefferson (Kurland and Lerner 1987, vol. 1: 647). Madison thought on the contrary that they would be small enough to have vicious majority-versus-minority conflicts. He argued that the larger nation would not so readily be sundered by such vicious conflicts. Anyone who contemplates what life would have been in the Anti-Federalist strongholds of upstate New York must wonder that any theorist could suppose that the views and values within such a community could be held in common. The chief Anti-Federalists were communal elites, including two prosperous Anti-Federalist lawyers (John Lansing and Robert Yates) in the New York delegation to the Philadelphia Convention. Their interests were clearly not congruent with the interests of the less wealthy and less powerful members of their own communities. On this issue it appears Madison was right, Montesquieu wrong.

Furthermore, Montesquieu thought coalitions of interests could not work; Madison thought they could, or at least he thought they could when they had complementary capacities so that they could gain mutual advantage from coordination and cooperation. The coalition that particularly concerned him was that of agrarian (especially plantation) producers and commercial shippers, financiers, and traders. Again, Madison was right, Montesquieu wrong, because, at least in important respects, this coalition worked remarkably well in creating and then managing a government.

In creating the larger nation Madison further attempted to design institutions that would prevent the national government from being arbitrary. The government he helped design has probably been the most successful major government in guaranteeing political and economic liberalism to most of its populace (slaves brutally excluded for three-quarters of a century and women almost completely excluded for more than a century). Part of the cost of that success is that that government is remarkably often incapable of addressing some problems – most notably, the problems of slavery, race, and poverty, but also perhaps violent crime in a society that has such burdens of race and poverty.

Madison's core ideas are often about how to deal with the peculiar situation of the 13 American states. This is not a broadly generalizable problem. Its solution does not even apply to some of the later federations of states, such as the Argentine federation, the Yugoslav federation of quasi-autonomous states, the Belgian quasi-federation, or the Soviet and Indian empire federations. It would be only moderately applicable to the Canadian and Australian federations. But of all the great liberal thinkers, Madison was the most effective. When he went head to head with the Anti-Federalist exponents of Montesquieu's views during the ratification debates, he won the day. He won the intellectual debate overwhelmingly, and he and the Federalists won the political debate by sometimes narrow margins but still with finality.

A distinctive difference between Madison and the major philosophers of liberalism, from Locke to Smith, is that Madison was foremost engaged in the effort to *create* a liberal government. He was not primarily a theorist and his was less a theoretical than a practical contribution, although one can claim that he was a better sociologist than Montesquieu and one of the best practical economists of his age. One might reasonably doubt that Locke, Smith, and Montesquieu could have done as successful a job of designing a constitution in Philadelphia as Madison did. He was – admittedly on the evidence of his own notes of the proceedings – apparently a master politician who was ready to tack and trim to get the best results feasible from his roomful of fellow conventioneers. Most of the others, on his record, seem to have been foremost concerned with their own idiosyncratic issues or with the issues most dear to their own states. This fact may have served the new nation and Madison well, because these men generally focused on side issues of representation of their states in the new order and on the painful issue of slavery.

While most of these men (excepting the few Anti-Federalists) likely shared Madison's concern with free trade within the states and with the economic liberalism that would allow commerce to prosper, they might have balked at giving the commerce power to the federal government if they had put enough effort into thinking through the longer-run consequences of this limited power. Those consequences included the growth of American government into an astonishingly powerful agency capable of governing without careful attention to constitutional constraints. Beginning with moves to control the growth of monopoly power and with corruption in federal agencies in the last quarter of the nineteenth century, and climaxing with the massive growth of administrative agencies to oversee much of the national economy in the New Deal era of the 1930s, the US government essentially invented an extraconstitutional fourth branch of government. That branch is the independent agencies which, taken together, are now by far the largest part of the government and possibly the most powerful of the four branches, at least in domestic matters. They are also remarkably autonomous from general political control and almost entirely independent of democratic control.

Perhaps the principal difference between Madison and the other liberal theorists is this. Virtually every major social theory issues in an institution or a set of institutions, although the move from social theory to institutions is commonly left open and is spelled out only in the roughest terms. Madison's theory issued in an actual set of institutions that were surprisingly subtle and adept from the beginning. They worked on the ground and remade the nation over which they governed. Those institutions were, of course, far more effective than any theory could have been, because they actually governed further relationships. Once they were in place, social theory could largely be laid aside and government would work reasonably well without it.

Of course, those institutions were theoretically grounded, better so than many of the conventioneers could have understood and certainly better so than the large number of people (only about 15 percent of those eligible) who voted on delegates to the state conventions that considered ratification of that constitution could possibly have understood. Among the great strengths of those institutions, once established, is that they give people stable expectations of the kind that Hobbes wanted government to provide. If the state protects me against attacks by others, I can expect my efforts on my own or my family's behalf to pay off.

Stable expectations are also of central importance in political liberalism. The obverse of stable expectations in political rule is arbitrariness. One of the strongest passages in the entire *Federalist Papers* is that in *Federalist* 47 in which Madison quotes Montesquieu on the claim that the arbitrary exercise of power is the core of tyranny. For Montesquieu, the point of separation of powers between the legislative, executive, and judicial branches is to reduce the odds of the arbitrariness that might follow from having any one of the branches fully in control (Montesquieu [1748] 1989 (book 11, ch. 6): 157). The argument is essentially the claim that requiring multiple branches to act to deprive one of liberty adds to one's security through regression toward the mean. It is far less likely that two or three branches will coordinate in an arbitrary suppression of someone's liberties than that a unified single branch will be arbitrary. Madison added to this view a somewhat more active vision of the roles of different parts of the government. They would be jealous of each other and would block each other's usurpations. Deep distrust would keep the parts of the government under control.

European Comparisons

In other nations, the effort to block the political and economic abuses of royal or other government prerogative has typically come as a reform of an extant form of government and has been accomplished through the very institutions of that government. In the United States, the "reform" was accomplished by the creation de novo of a liberal government, the first avowedly liberal government of a major nation. It was also arguably the weakest, least intrusive government in a major nation of its time. The documents and practices that make up the English constitution include some, such as the Magna Carta, that restrict governmental power. The US Constitution simultaneously created a government and greatly restricted its power. Other essentially de novo governments, such as the French, Russian, and Chinese revolutionary regimes, were created with a mandate to do things, including the extensive reconstruction of the society. The US history is nearly unique in the de novo creation of deliberately constrained and limited government. One might say the US Constitution eviscerated government except that there was no prior government to eviscerate, with the partial exception of the governments of the individual 13 states. Some of these states, such as Pennsylvania and Virginia, had largely abnegated some of the intrusive tariff powers that wrecked the development of the nascent US economy before the Constitution. But others, such as New York and tiny Rhode Island, often exercised such powers with a vengeance and they hamstrung the larger nation.

Because of these distinctive differences Anthony King (2000) speaks of American exceptionalism in the American attitude of distrust in government. He further argues that ordinary Europeans (as opposed to European academic social scientists) do not even conceive of government in the way Americans do. For Americans, the government is not just the current administration or some agent. It is all of those bureaucrats and their power in Washington, now and in the past and into the future. For Europeans, the phrase "the government" means the current regime of Tony Blair, Gerhard Schröder, or Silvio Berlusconi. The government is something that can be thrown out and replaced with something different and maybe even better. To Americans, it is something that has been there a couple of centuries and will continue very possibly for many more centuries. Throwing it out would be pointless because it would only be replaced by another. The best we can do is to hem it in as much as possible.

In the light of King's account, however, it is interesting that Montesquieu thought of England as the nation with a proper distrust of government in his time. The English government evolved over time, becoming less parasitic as the king's prerogatives were increasingly curtailed. By the time of the twentieth century, the dominant view of government in the UK must have become relatively sanguine: the government was largely there to serve the public. No one other than the royal family and some retainers could have thought most European governments of preceding centuries were there to serve them. Governments were established as entities that then, through military action, established the state's boundaries, and the subjects of the state were just that: subjects. Their chief value to the state was as sources of revenue. Napoleon dramatically altered the relationship by building his massive armies out of citizens rather than out of mercenaries. The need for large numbers of soldiers who might actually be loyal profoundly changed the relationship between citizens and their government. Hence, the invention of modern nationalist warfare sped the development of political liberties and of democracy, which in turn further enabled modern warfare.

King notes that many Europeans may come to have an American view of the government of the European Union, which has been created de novo much as the United States was in 1787–9. Europeans already seem to refer to Brussels much the way Americans refer to Washington, as the somewhat distasteful seat of a bureaucratic and at best faintly necessary government. The French and the Dutch rejected the EU constitution on grounds that are largely incoherent, with both immigrants and racist opponents of immigration voting against it. The political phrasing of the issues in Europe is distorted almost beyond recognition in the supposition that what is at stake is the creation of great power in Brussels.

What has chiefly happened so far is the reduction of power of all government by freeing commerce of the petty intrusions of the individual nations. It looks very much like the US experience and its Commerce Clause. The Commerce Clause probably had the effect of reducing antipathy to government in the early United States because it reduced the power of government to intrude in people's lives. The English opposition to Brussels has successfully distorted the issue into one of distrust in the European supragovernment, as though their own national government were beyond such distrust. For many issues, Madison's sense of the capriciousness and destructiveness of the individual American states' governments just as well fit the individual European national governments.

Even debates over a uniform currency, the euro, have been infected with this distortion. Opponents of the EU have also somewhat successfully raised chauvinist objections to turning over the domestic currency to a central government. An indifferent economist surveying monetary policy in many of these and in very many other nations would recommend taking such policy out of the hands of national politicians, who all too often cannot be trusted with such policy, both because they lack any competent understanding of what monetary policy does for – or to – the society and because they have personal political interests in misusing such policy.

A side benefit of the new European state is that, in addition to bringing greater liberalism in commerce, it has also brought dramatically greater freedom to individuals in their activities and movements in Europe. This seems to be an especially clear case of the interaction between economic and political freedoms.

Perhaps the most theoretical among the opponents of European government have in mind not what is currently on the agenda but rather the possible logic of the longer-run future of that government. For this concern, of course, the US experience is not promising for those who value relatively weak government. The US government is probably still weaker domestically than the governments of many other industrial states. Its seeming power to various critics may be more nearly the effect of its massive and innovative economy and its brutally powerful military. But that government is almost inconceivably powerful in comparison to what Madison and the Philadelphia conventioneers thought they were creating.

To win the argument over whether Montesquieu-like small republics or large and diverse states are the better defenders of liberties, both economic and political, probably requires a discussion of more than merely domestic arrangements. The question is whether life in North America would have been harsher if it had been carved into small republics. The view of early leaders of the European movement, such as Jean Monnet, was clearly that peace and prosperity depended on transcending small states' interests by a merger of those states into a European suprastate. If, as seems likely, economic and political liberties interact so that securing either helps to secure the other, then the European Union may be generally liberating even in such ways as to undercut the current wave of quasi-communitarian subnationalist movements.

Power Inequality and Trust

Chapter 2 raised issues of how any citizen could know enough about government officials in general to be able to trust them on any of the three standard theories of trust, all of which depend on assessments of the trustworthiness of the agent to be trusted or distrusted. That chapter also briefly raised the problem of power differentials as an obstacle to trust. Large power differences undercut motivations of trustworthiness to act on behalf of another. For most of us most of the time, the most powerful agency we face is government, especially national government in a state with a powerful government. The first of these issues – citizens' knowledge – is elaborated in chapter 3 in the discussion of survey research; the second – government's great power – belongs here in the account of liberal distrust of government, which is historically distrust of the ways it uses its power.

If we need or want to cooperate with someone or with a commercial entity, typically we have choices or options available. If my experience with you is not good or if your reputation is not good, I can most likely find someone else to deal with. We commonly do not have such choices with respect to government and its agents. To get choice, we might even have to emigrate. For example, if we earn a living in the United States we have to deal with the Internal Revenue Service (IRS) or in the United Kingdom with the Inland Revenue. In the theory of Karen Cook and Richard Emerson (Emerson 1962, 1964; Cook and Emerson 1978), the mere impossibility of switching to alternative partners gives those we deal with greater power over us than is suggested merely by their roles. The fact that we are forced to deal with this single agency for certain important matters means that it has enormous power over us. We do not have even vaguely similar power over it, so that we suffer from power dependence. This means that we cannot trust these powerful institutions, or that at least the possibility of trusting them is severely undercut, especially in the encapsulated interest sense of trust, because my power dependence undermines any hope I might have to get you to reciprocally cooperate with me (see Cook, Hardin, and Levi 2005, ch. 3; Farrell 2004).

This is not the theory of Madison, but it fits his theory. Had he articulated this problem, his own theory might have been better grounded, but he clearly enough saw the implications of governmental power, as anyone should be able to see them. In the Cook and Emerson account, however, *the impossibility of trust is built into the unequal relationship* and there is nothing we can do to make governmental agents entirely trustworthy with respect to their roles over us. Some of them may be imbued with the spirit of public service and they might, if we only knew it, be trustworthy in their dealings with us. Even these agents cannot be trusted by most citizens in the sense of any of the three standard theories of trust. For the encapsulated interest theory, they do not encapsulate our interests, they merely work according to the norms of their roles. They know little about any of us and we know as little about them. For the moral and dispositional accounts of trustworthiness, these agents could be relatively trustworthy, but you and I are not likely to be in a position to know that.

In the case of the IRS in the US, we actually have been given a lot of information about their responsible behavior because Congress, in one of its recently nasty moods, libeled it and subjected its agents to extensive oversight. The result was, contrary to the supposed beliefs of the self-serving, grandstanding members of Congress, to clear the names of the accused IRS agents. Of course, for most Americans who even noticed the attacks on the IRS, the learning probably stopped at the front page coverage of the false accusations and was not corrected by the much later stories in the back pages of the exoneration of these agents and of the IRS in general.

Even if we suppose that these agents are likely to be public-spirited, or at least obedient to the norms of their roles, we still can conclude that citizens are in the weak position of being power dependent on these agents. Of course, citizens are arguably even more power dependent on the elected officials who write the grossly unequal tax laws of recent American legislation. In principle the citizens could turn all of these officials out of office at the next election. Instead, they are likely to return virtually all of them to office election after election. In the 2004 elections in the US, 99 percent of incumbents running for reelection to the House of Representatives (with 435 members) outside of Texas were reelected.[33] The voters commonly say in surveys that Congress is somewhere toward the rotten end of the spectrum of approval, but acting together, they repeatedly send those people back to office to fester for another two years (there are many efforts to explain this seeming anomaly; see, for example, Hibbing and Theiss-Morse 2002).[34] Probably no other electorate is as craven as that in the US, but everywhere incumbency seems to be relatively protected.

Concluding Remarks

Because of the intensity of the debates at the time of the US Constitution and the high quality of the exegesis of opposing sides in the *Federalist Papers* and in the writings of the Anti-Federalists, it is possible that the American populace of that moment better understood the grounds of liberalism than they have at any other time, before or since. The exciting debates in eastern Europe from 1989 until a few years later may similarly have educated more people to a good understanding of these issues than in any other society since the era of the constitutional debates in the US. And the debates around 2005 over the ratification of the EU constitutional treaty probably raised public interest and understanding to unusual levels, especially in the nations – such as France – in which the decision is made in popular referendums.[35]

One might suppose it would be good to have such understanding in other times as well. But that is a far too demanding hope, because the intensity of debates around 1787, 1989 and 2005 necessarily depended on the fact that the debates were potentially going to affect how we organized our national lives. In most eras, this is simply not true in any such significant way. In a sense therefore, the constitutional generation's wisdom and understanding dies with it. Indeed, it probably already dies in the politics of the new institutions once these are in place, as in a sad sense it did for Madison himself. After the new government was in place, Madison became foremost a pragmatic politician focused on the issues of the day and on the machinations that could best secure quotidian victories for his side. He created the first US political party despite his claim in *Federalist* 10 that the scale of the American polity would prevent the rise of such a large faction. Several of the charismatic liberals of eastern Europe have suffered even sharper declines in their own apparent understandings once new or reformed institutions were put in place. For the peoples of eastern Europe, it is already politics as usual – even though there had not been such "usual" politics for generations before 1989.

What residue of the constitutional debates is left as a live political force or idea? In the US, perhaps primarily the aura of distrust in government. Any failure of major policies is almost instantly attributed to the incapacity of government to overcome petty interest-group or individual incentives. The Vietnam war, for example, demolished half a generation's expectations that government might be both benign and sensible. The partial failure of programs on poverty and racism are viewed cynically as the naturally low expectation of government will and capacity, even though for a brief period government action on these problems was seen as admirable. If King is right, there may be no such residue in Europe, although change may be on the way. The instant antipathy to the growth of the European Union in England, and later surprisingly in France and the Netherlands, sounds very much like the American distrust of government.

In the United States, as in the United Kingdom, deep distrust of government has more consistently characterized conservative than liberal thought. Ironically, however, conservatives have been very quick to trumpet the merits and commitments of governments under Ronald Reagan, Margaret Thatcher, and George W. Bush. As the war in Iraq has seemingly demonstrated the relative incompetence of government to carry out its ambitious program there, conservatives have been slow to return to their usually critical stance. John Tierney (2004) asks how did "so many conservatives, who normally don't trust their government to run a public school down the street, come to believe that federal bureaucrats could transform an entire nation in the alien culture of the Middle East?"

Finally, note an instructive way to see the Madisonian vision of restrictions on government. In a story of his being deceived by a student who wanted a grade for a course *before* finishing a required paper, Piotr Sztompka (1999: 38) gets the issue entirely right in his sly observation that "rules, codes, and regulations may sometimes embody the collective wisdom about the average trustworthiness of people." This is a richly Humean view. The rules at the university where Sztompka taught that student barred his giving her a grade before she finished her paper. The rules were right in her case – after getting her grade she never did the paper.

Many of us commonly have optimistic expectations of the behavior of others, including, of course, government officials. But the constitutional constraints we have put in the way of action by these officials very likely embody an important bit of collective wisdom that may seldom be seen or fully understood by individuals; and those institutions protect citizens against their failure of vision. Distrust came relatively easily to people, such as the liberal theorists of distrust and many of the citizens of the former Soviet Union and of Communist eastern Europe (see e.g. Sajo 1999), who had lived with earlier governments' abuses and who wanted to block them in their own lives. The liberal theory of distrust is an important body of collective wisdom and the institutions it has produced are the embodiment of that distrust.

8

Representative Democracy and Trust

This book opened with the observation that over the past decade or so trust has become a major worry of many scholars and pundits. The reason for their concern is the widely accepted view that trust and social capital are in decline in the United States and in several other advanced democracies, including Canada, Sweden, and the United Kingdom (but see Ladd 1996; Portes and Landolt 1996). Many scholars think that the trends in large survey data show both declining trust in government and in our fellow citizens as individuals. It would be perverse to find declining trust in governments of nations that were formerly fascist or otherwise autocratic and widely abusive of their own peoples, and indeed the trends in Italy, Germany, and Japan do not mirror those in the North Atlantic community.

Much of the current wave of work on trust in the advanced democratic societies has been directed at understanding apparent changes in trust over time (see, for example, Pharr and Putnam 2000; Sztompka 1999). The urge is to explain at the margin. In some ways, the work of Locke, Hume, Smith, and Madison, among the most important inventors of liberalism, is at the core of how society works rather than about marginal changes. They were concerned with the foundations of a working society with good government. The argument in contemporary debate is roughly as stated by Geraint Parry (1976: 134): "Political trust is an epiphenomenon of social trust [which is trust between individual citizens]. Where consensus is lacking, social trust and consequently political trust will be lacking and the political system will be less stable." Although it is often asserted, this claim of the spilling over of trust at one level to trust at other levels is not well demonstrated or even much addressed empirically. A version of it was articulated by Gabriel Almond and Sidney Verba (1965: 228): "Belief in the benignity of one's fellow citizen is directly related to one's propensity to join with others in political activity. General social trust is translated into politically relevant trust."

One can at least imagine that a populace among whom there is fairly strong distrust could nevertheless have confidence in their government or that people who are quite optimistic about each other would distrust their government. Indeed, the former seems to be the finding of Almond and Verba (1965: 229) from survey research in Germany and Italy. It would also seem to be the virtually self-evident fact of Madison and many of his associates that they trusted each other fairly extensively even while they constitutionally distrusted the government that they created and would soon staff. Indeed, one might well argue that wariness toward government could enhance the development of personal trust relationships, as in the world of samizdat in the Soviet Union.

An elitist response to widespread distrust by the populace is to suppose that participation should not be encouraged so that the better educated and more politically active citizens, who tend to be much more trusting, run the government. Mill ([1861] 1977) seems to have held a version of this view. On Russell Neuman's (1986: 3–4) account, those who know enough to be able to judge much of the government trustworthy might be only about 5 percent of the American electorate. (The fraction must be higher in Israel and perhaps intermediate in several European nations.) Orlando Patterson (1999: 185) says that this small group, who are attentive and active, "accounts for the vibrancy and integrity of the democratic system in America." If so, a few activists go a long way toward making democracy be responsive to the much larger number of those who are distrusting. That would be a possible but also an odd result. It is also odd to think that

Madison and his peers distrusted government in principle, while the masses today, who evidently distrust government, may well distrust it because it is elite. Hence, the elite salvation of government might in fact be the elite capture of government.

Parry (1976: 136) concludes sensibly that it is possible "that political trust is not so much rooted in social attitudes as consequent upon the effective performance of certain political institutions." Arguably, this view fits the contemporary American experience of apparently declining confidence in government (see various contributions to Pharr and Putnam 2000; Hardin 2002b). Perhaps it also fits recent changes in eastern Europe, especially the Czech Republic, Hungary, and Poland. During the decade after 1989, Poles for example went from immediate euphoria to distress as the effects of the transition were at first fairly harsh economically, and then back to optimism as the reforms, both political and economic, began to work positively (Sztompka 1999: 151–90). It should be no surprise that an initial transition from central to market allocation is costly in the short run because it undercuts systems that, even if inefficient, did produce and deliver goods. Getting new institutions for the market in place cannot be instantaneous. The change could also not seem entirely certain to work, so that people might tend to game the changes in the short term, making profits where they can. This fits Sztompka's and liberal theorists' concern with stable expectations. It takes time to develop stability and in the interim people have weak grounds for confidence that is grounded in expectations of reliability. Several of the eastern nations now have reason to harbor relatively optimistic expectations.

Extreme distrust in a society is said to favor hegemony (Dahl 1971: 150–2). One might sooner claim that hegemony, especially autocratic hegemony, favors extreme distrust between citizens even as a matter of deliberate policy in order to keep them from coalescing into oppositional groups. Such individual-level distrust was a chronic symptom of Soviet life under Stalin. Distrust of government seems to be a better way to go. Parry says "it is still open for someone to hold, with Hume, that such distrust is an excellent working hypothesis in politics" (Parry 1976: 139). This appears to be Parry's own view, as suggested by his criticisms of the many authors who seem to deplore distrust in government. I think it is a correct working hypothesis, largely for Hume's reasons of risk aversion where the downside of misplaced trust is disastrous, while the loss from distrust cannot be anywhere near as disastrous. (For individual-level trust, this asymmetry is not likely to be true in general. Indeed, in a relatively decent society, distrust will likely cost more through lost opportunities than misplaced trust would cost from losses through deception (see further, Hardin 2002b, ch. 5).) In the past century, it seems likely that no polity trusted its government more than Soviet citizens did for the decades of Stalin's rule and that no large industrial polity has been more abused by its government. For epistemological reasons, trust in government probably cannot be justified even when the government is a good one, but distrust can be justified (Hardin 1999c).

Locke held that society turns power over to its governors, "whom society hath set over it self, with this express or tacit Trust, That it shall be imployed for their good, and the preservation of their Property" (Locke [1690] 1988 (§171): 381). Locke's vision has not held sway over either theorists or practitioners. But there are widely held views that citizens must trust government if government is to work well and that a reputed decline in citizen trust of government bodes ill for many contemporary democratic societies. Madison and other federalists designed the US Constitution on the contrary principle that government must be distrusted and should therefore be constrained in many ways to prevent it from abusing citizens.

Against the Lockean thesis even at a conceptual level, it is relatively clear that, if it is not possible for most people to claim in a strong sense that they trust major organizations, then they also cannot claim in that sense to trust government. Most of us cannot sensibly claim to have the knowledge required for establishing the trustworthiness of government officials, agencies, or government generally. Therefore, we cannot trust them. We might learn specific bits of knowledge of their actions and apparent incentives that seem sufficient to distrust particular officials and whole agencies (Montinola 2004), but we cannot so readily amass the body of knowledge necessary to trust very many, if any, of them.

Democratic Theory

Why might government competence be declining in some advanced democracies? The claim of communitarians and many others is that the people have changed and are therefore more skeptical of government because the social organization of our lives has changed (Etzioni and Diprete 1979). There may be some element of truth in this claim (but see Newton and Norris 2000). Others suppose that styles of politicians have changed, as in the shift from traditional campaigning to the marketing of candidates, especially via television (Manin 1997). I will focus on a quite different causal nexus to argue that *the underlying political issues have changed* in ways that reduce confidence in government.

There have been two mutually exacerbating changes in the nature of public policy issues in recent decades. The first is a systematic, big shock: the essential end, at least for the near term after Reagan and Thatcher, of the central focus on the management of the economy for production and distribution. The second change is the slow and steady rise during the postwar era of issues that are systematically unrelated to each other and often complex. Together, these two changes entail that the organization of politics along a roughly left–right economic dimension is no longer plausible. Those coming of political age over the past generation in the advanced democracies generally might not recognize the political organization that prevailed for the preceding generations and even centuries in many of these countries. Their concerns are a hotchpotch of unrelated issues that are not the obvious domain of any traditional political party. The era of fundamental simplicity in the statement of the main political issue has passed, at least for now.

Perhaps the fundamental problem we face is therefore an ongoing redefinition of democratic politics and participation. Democracy has been recreated in new forms many times. When democracy shifted from small to larger societies it therefore had to become representative instead of direct democracy. Later, representative democracy shifted from the selection of representatives by lot, by random choice, as in Athens and Renaissance Venice, to elections. Choice by election has long since turned politicians into a professional class (Manin 1997). At about the same time democracy shifted from more or less free-for-all elections to party-dominated contests. There were reasons at the time to think each of these changes was somehow bad and tended toward less democracy. But at some level, it would be hard to say that any of these moves was a mistake because they were virtually necessitated by social circumstances. A nation of 50 or 300 million people cannot be run the way a small city-state, such as Athens or Venice, was run.

We may have entered another transitional era, with democracy shifting from coherent, party-dominated contests to free-for-all elections of a new kind in which the competence of citizens to judge candidates and issues may be in decline (even, perhaps, in their own view) because the complexity and diversity of issues make them extremely difficult to understand and package. Yet citizens' reduced confidence might not be worrisome. To some extent, *we are losing confidence in government precisely because we no longer think we need it in the important realm of the economy.* We evidently had more confidence in government when it was trying to manage the economy, but arguably without much success. It was ideology, not science that gave us confidence.

In the US, national party commitment to social libertarianism has also passed. One of the most dramatic changes in party definition in all of US history is suggested by the Republican party's nomination of Barry Goldwater in 1964 and its nomination of George W. Bush in 2000. Goldwater was perhaps the most firmly social libertarian candidate ever selected by any major party, although he was only more socially libertarian in degree than most twentieth-century Republican choices.[36] Bush is one of the most antilibertarian major-party candidates in American history. He is possibly rivaled by William Jennings Bryan, who was also a determined Christian. In Tennessee's infamous Monkey trial Bryan argued the case for the prosecution of the teacher, John Thomas Scopes, who had taught the theory of evolution. But

Bryan was nominated three times by the Democratic party, which – at least since the Civil War – has never been centrally concerned with social liberties.

The change from Goldwater to Bush must be utterly demoralizing to any social libertarian, whether in the tradition of John Stuart Mill or Immanuel Kant. With the rise of the social agenda in the Republican party, there is no longer any substantial voice for social libertarianism in the US. Fifty years ago one would have said that the US was the home of social libertarianism. Today there is no such strong home for it anywhere, but several European parties have livelier libertarian politics.

There appears to be much sharper ideological debate now when there is also broad agreement on what used to be the central divisive issue: letting the economy more or less run itself. In the US neither Democrats nor Republicans and in the UK neither Conservatives nor Labour seriously want to attempt central control over the economy. In earlier times, the party of business wanted mercantilist control of the economy on behalf of business, with high tariffs to block competition from imports; today it wants something closer to laissez faire, although particular industries and firms would be happy to receive government-mandated benefits so long as these do not go to everyone but only to, for example, steel, textiles, or agricultural products. Earlier, the Democratic party wanted far-reaching control over the economy; today it works for modest welfare programs that can be funded from the gains of a fairly free-wheeling economy. It is an interesting question why the American national parties have become so ideological just now when the old basis of their ideological split is no longer an issue, but that is another story. The death of social libertarianism in the Republican party is only part of that story.

The focus of politics

In 1910 the American Medical Association released the Flexner Report about medical education (Flexner 1910). Along the way, the report concluded that sometime about the beginning of the twentieth century, going to an American doctor finally was more likely to benefit someone who was ill than to harm them. This poses an odd thought. George Washington and several British kings may have been killed or at least hastened to death by their doctors when they bled the great men to remove evil humors from their bodies. The people who did not have access to doctors in their time might, other things equal, have lived longer than those who did have access.

The political scientist John Mueller (1999) argues that economic theory has reached a similar state to that of medicine in 1900. Going to an economist might now generally more often be helpful to governmental policy-makers than harmful. The main advice of economists today in many nations is to leave the economy alone to a substantial degree and to let the market work. It is, of course, a corollary of letting the market run its course without massive government planning of economic growth and distribution that government escapes the burden of being judged for the success or failure of its economic planning. Of course, while this may be true at least in principle, the public may not get the point. Although economic performance was once the main dimension on which the major parties divided in many democratic societies, today it is increasingly a dimension on which they agree. They disagree about various welfare programs, but these are a small part of the national budget.

If Mueller is right, this sounds like a good change. Governments are getting at least this main economic issue roughly right. But at the same time *many other political issues have changed* in ways that reduce confidence in government.

For most of the history of modern democracy, politics has been organized around economic issues. Indeed, the central worry of many of the authors of the first system of broad democracy, under the US Constitution, was the threat that genuine democracy posed to property and its privileges. In earlier periods the economic conflict took fairly specific substantive form in support for particular interests against others, such as landed estates and plantations against manufacturing and urban interests. It eventually became a more abstract conflict between the state and the market (especially in Europe) or between business in general and other groups (especially in the United States). Japan has been an anomaly

with its near consensus on essentially mercantilist management of the economy for the benefit of industry and agricul-
ture with no antistatist party. Its peculiarly deep and lasting
economic difficulties in the 1990s arguably derive primarily
from its past mercantilist policies and the incapacity of its
virtually hegemonic mercantilist-statist party to jettison
those policies and reduce the role of the state in running
the economy.

The economic conflict had a domestic and an international
form: greater equality versus untrammeled liberty, communism versus the free market. The institutional form of the
domestic issue was central planning versus laissez faire. The
issue was never quite that simple, of course, because, for
example, a typical corporation wanted regulatory, subsidy,
and tariff policies that would specifically benefit it against
a fully free-wheeling market; industrial workers wanted
job and wage protection; professional groups wanted restrictive licensing and regulation; farmers everywhere have
wanted subventions, some variant of price supports, and protection against imports of food; and all of these groups have
often wanted more competition among the other groups.
Extant corporations may now have become more laissez-faire
than they ever would have wanted, because upstart corporations often thrive in competition with the older ones. The
general movement to increased laissez faire has not been
equally quick in all of the advanced democracies, but the
trend is generally similar in all but perhaps Japan, in part
because of the globalization of firms and loosening of trade
restrictions.

Now we seem to be in an era in which the economic division is no longer crucial because we have reached near-
consensus on how to handle the main economic problems.
We generally handle them by letting them handle themselves.
With the passing of the division on economics, there is no
similarly cogent simple dimension on which to organize the
contest for political leadership. We may have to deal with
economic crises in the future and we may disagree on how
to do that. But, to lesser extent in some of the advanced
democracies than in others, we seem to have accepted basic
reliance on the market and have increasingly given up on
central planning to organize our economic prospects.

The former left–right antagonism has been reduced to a very short spread from those who prefer more generous welfare programs to those who prefer somewhat less generous programs, and the difference in the two positions is a very small fraction of national income in any given nation – although the difference between France and either the UK or the US is substantial. Radical reorganization of the economy to achieve some degree of equality or fairness is now virtually off the agenda. Often, perhaps because the causal relations are not well understood, the split on welfare policy seems to be as much a matter of tone as of content. For many people, it is a difference that is easily trumped by formerly minor concerns such as items in the social agenda and regional preferences. The odd result is that politics may be noisier and seemingly more intense and even bitter, but it is less important. The rise in volume may be a temporary, transitional phenomenon. We will not know for sure until we first live with politics over marginal issues for a longer period. Just possibly, people have the social capital as well as the leisure time to organize intensely on marginal issues. Also just possibly they are inane enough to do so to the neglect of more far-reaching issues.

The European story is somewhat more sharply drawn than the North American because it hangs very much on the fact that there had been socialist and even communist parties in Europe. These were partly tarnished by the economic failure of communism in the East. That failure was itself a consequence of government incapacity to plan and run an increasingly complex high-tech economy, in which entrepreneurial creativity seems to be crucially important. That part of an economy evidently cannot be run well by central authorities; it must be allowed to run on its own if it is to prosper. How can one tell teenagers to go out and create a new industry as Steve Jobs, Bill Gates, and others recently did and as William Hewlett and David Packard did a generation earlier? With their former central agendas essentially dead, the European parties of the left may follow the lead of the American Democratic and Republican parties and become politically vague and opportunistic rather than clearly directed. Such leaders as Tony Blair and Gerhard Schröder personally have followed

Bill Clinton's path of unsystematic policy, often at the cost of rankling the older socialists of their parties.

Citizens

Two oddly contradictory claims are made of citizens' actual trust in government. They are said not to trust government in general but typically to trust the individual agents of government with whom they personally have dealings (Klein 1994). Contrariwise, they are said to think all politicians are scoundrels but nevertheless to think government works well for them. The latter view fits with Hume's point that we design government to work even if it is staffed by knaves. The former fits any conception of trust that holds that it depends on ongoing relationships. These two contradictory claims are largely subjective, and the survey data that lie behind them suffer from a weakness that is probably inherent in survey research on relatively complex issues. We would first have to explain how they should think of trust, or we would have to ask relatively complex questions that, in sum, could get to a stable and meaningful notion of trust. As in the problem of assessing whether there has been a decline in trust over the past several decades, these claims about citizen trust of government are severely underarticulated.

The relation of citizens to government in general is not a relation of trust or distrust. At best, much of the time it is a relationship of inductive expectations and acquiescence (Hardin 1999c). Obviously, what citizens must want of government is that it be trustworthy – even though citizens cannot know that it is, at least not in a strong enough sense for them to trust it. In a democracy, citizens can vote from their limited knowledge of government and can therefore affect what it does. Such control can be important even without citizen trust in government.

In the end, trust may still be crucial to the success of government, but in one way that has been discussed almost not at all, and in another way that has not been a main focus in the trust-and-government literature. First, trust *within* the government might be far more important in government by junta than in democratic government. Second, those most attentive to government will also be those most likely to know enough about governmental actions and structures to know whether the government and its agents are trustworthy. If they are also the people most likely to oppose government in response to its failings, then the possibility of trustworthiness and the epistemological possibility of trust could be fundamentally important to the stability of government. The significance of their role in support of government might be ramified by the implicit support of those who act from mere expectations without articulate knowledge of the trustworthiness of government. The expectations of the latter group might be based in large part on the expectations of others, just as most of us know many of the things we know only in the sense that we gather that others think those things are true.

Unfortunately, if this is the role of trust in supporting government, there is little reason to think that the interests of those knowledgeable enough about certain agents or agencies of government to judge them trustworthy would correlate with the interests of most citizens. Trust within the government might make cooperative policy efforts easier, but that is independent of citizen trust of government, and the efforts it might make easier could be awful for most citizens.

Citizens perhaps justifiably lack confidence in government to handle many of the issues of importance today. Yet, citizens who supposed they could do things better than their governors did them have voted, in US referendums, to adopt policies with unexpected grim consequences. In many cases of policy-making by referendum, arguably, the citizenry are misled or they mislead themselves to believe the issues are far simpler than they are and they vote simplistically. Consider two examples, one very briefly because it is funny but not grim, and another at greater length because it is depressingly grim. The two examples are peculiarly American – indeed they fit the view that many people in other nations hold that American politics is uniquely bizarre.

California's Proposition 3 in 1998 proposed to correct a blunder by the state that might have kept its delegates from being seated at national party conventions. An earlier law had made the primaries open, but the national parties sensibly do not permit delegates chosen in open (that is, nonparty) primaries to vote in their conventions. Unfortunately, the proposition to correct this blunder was too intricate for voters, who killed it, although it seems implausible that a majority of voters meant to force California out of the national conventions that select presidential candidates. State officials thwarted the supposedly popular will by distorting the process in ways that would let California delegates be seated in the conventions of the year 2000 (*New York Times*, Nov. 15, 1998, sec. 1).[37] At some level, this was not even a difficult choice for anyone to understand; it was merely made difficult by a blunder in the writing of the proposition.

Now turn to a deplorable and very important example. On Susan Estrich's (1998: 74) account, the California referendum that brought in the clumsy and finally very destructive three-strikes policy on dealing with repeat felons was grossly misconceived, and yet it was enormously popular. That law requires mandatory longer prison sentences for felons with at least one prior conviction for a serious or violent felony. "The result of mandatory laws and punishment by slogan," Estrich observes, "is that we spend more and more money locking up less and less violent people." In an early case to which the new law was applied, a one-slice pizza thief was sentenced to a term of 25 years to life for his "felony petty theft," with no possibility of parole before serving at least 20 years (*New York Times*, Mar. 5, 1995).

The California law was a response to the kidnapping and murder of a young girl, Polly Klaas, by Richard Alan Davis, a recently released kidnapper. The popular outcry over that murder led to a referendum requiring harsh longer sentences for felons with at least one prior conviction for a serious or violent felony. The law does not require that the new crime be violent and it barred judges from assessing the dangerousness of the person committing the crime. The law lumps minor felons and kidnap-murderers together as people who should live out much of their lives in jail in order to protect society.

Ironically, Davis was originally serving a mandatory maximum 16-year sentence for a prior kidnapping. He was released after only eight years under a California law that *cut in half* all sentences of those already then in jail in order to make more room in the prisons for newly convicted offenders, including petty drug offenders as perhaps the largest group. That law did not distinguish how violent were the crimes of those to be released (Massing 1998). Of course, the three-strikes law that was adopted by referendum increased the problem of overcrowding in prisons that provoked the release of Davis, which led to Polly's murder.

Governor George Pataki of New York has dealt with similar problems in his state by sensibly releasing minor drug offenders in order to make more room for violent offenders. He has done this quietly, perhaps because punishment by slogan would trump him if he were too assertive about the policy. For a lover of democracy, it is distressing to defend such discretionary action on the part of a public official contrary to popular will. But the nature of popular will on such complex issues is also distressing, as it would likely be even to an individual voter who could discuss the issues quietly rather than through sloganeering groups.

Here we should be less confident of the people than of the government. These two referendum issues were relatively simple, and yet they were too hard for voters to understand them well. This is not surprising if we suppose, as rational choice theorists since Anthony Downs (1957) do, that voters have little incentive to vote and therefore even less incentive to understand how to vote their interests (Hardin 2000, 2002a). As the complexity of policy increases, and as the electorate grows larger, these considerations weigh more heavily and militate against the expectation that the electorate will vote intelligently. Moreover, as issues become in many ways more diverse, so that there is little hope of a coherent party alignment as in the formerly neat division from economically conservative to economically liberal, the accountability of elected officials becomes increasingly murky. Governmental failures – as in many goals of the Great Society programs or in the Vietnam war in the United States, in elaborate welfare programs in Europe, and in complicated supports for farmers almost everywhere – however, are relatively clear even to generally ill-informed voters. Hence, voters may not know enough to vote well but they may often have compelling reason to think government is incompetent.

If an individual behaved as incoherently as the electorate and legislature of California in the three-strikes example, we would likely say that that individual was hopelessly irrational. Here is a brutally brief summary: because a kidnapper was released after only eight years under one cavalierly ill-conceived law, a pizza thief was incarcerated for at least 20 years under an even more cavalierly ill-conceived law.

Such issues as the environment, safety, and the social agenda of the religious right do not fit easily with the traditional political parties. The association of environmental policy with the left, at least in the United States, has followed for the accidental reason that the initial targets of environmental regulation were such corporations as electrical utilities, big steel, and the paper industry. But there is nothing inherent in the issue of environmental protection that is contrary to the interests of individuals from all points on the economic spectrum. It is natural therefore that environmental issues are attached to a separate party in the proportional representation system of Germany rather than to the traditional left or right parties.

A similar story can be told of the introduction of safety equipment on automobiles. American auto makers long opposed the introduction of airbags, while other, especially German and Swedish, manufacturers made complex airbag systems part of their sales appeal. It is very hard to see safety as a left–right issue. If anything, one might suppose the relatively less affluent, who are traditionally associated with the left, might be less in favor of such innovations than the more affluent. Indeed, as is also true of the less developed nations, the poor must typically see it as less in their interest than the well-off would to have environmental and safety regulations that generally raise costs (Hardin 1999b).

Finally, the attachment of the social agenda of the religious right to the Republican party in the United States, might seem natural today. But it would have seemed quite unlikely to an earlier generation who more readily saw the Democratic party as populist and the Republican party as far more nearly libertarian. William Jennings Bryan, one of the most grotesque of the populist backers of an early part of the social agenda, was a Democrat who, admittedly, had long since outlived his intelligence before he participated in the notorious

Scopes trial. Teddy Roosevelt, not quite a free-thinker and not likely sophisticated enough to know whether he was a libertarian, but still an individualist, was a Republican. The Republican party may have mortgaged its soul to the religious right in order to gain political success in the South after Lyndon Johnson, a southern Democrat, fought for civil rights.

In the face of such issues, we will not be able to hold office-holders accountable except for oddly assembled packages of positions on seemingly unrelated issues. And we may therefore conclude that our officials are incompetent and therefore untrustworthy because they cannot handle such complexity. Admittedly, politics over issue X is more perverse in the United States than in most nations, but contemporary issues in all the advanced democracies are messy and no longer fit the left–right economic dimension of the past century or centuries.

The success of economic policy, if it holds for much longer, may mean that citizens have less reason to suppose parties capture their interests in a summary way. Hence, they have one less clue for how to vote intelligently. It would be a saving grace if governmental policy matters less now than it once seemed to matter. If the economy can perform well without supposedly wise tinkering by government, and if we do not face other major crises, perhaps government will seem less important than it once did. But even then, its tasks may be so diverse and so complex that it must typically often fail in them, so that citizens continue to find it incompetent and, therefore, lack confidence in it. In the most sanguine scenario, the government of the next decade or so might enjoy the credit, falsely, for economic performance for which it has little responsibility. Once the reasons for economic prosperity are more fully understood, however, national leaders may no longer be able to win credit for that prosperity, as Clinton and a string of leaders of Japan's Liberal Democratic party have done. Leaders would then be judged by their supposed successes or failings on other issues.

What we face now is a transition to a way of aggregating ill-articulated preferences of those who cannot take the time to understand the issues being decided in their names well enough even to know their own preferences. We would want representatives to represent us in the sense of serving our interests (Hardin 2000). But we must want them to do that for us even in the face of the sad fact that we do not know what would serve our interests and we might judge our representatives harshly even for happening to serve us well merely because we do not understand that they do so.

Politicians

The two most successful politicians of our time have been Helmut Kohl and Ronald Reagan. Reagan escaped much of the burden of complexity because he predated the events of 1989 and partly took credit for them. In keeping with traditional political divisions, Reagan stood with Margaret Thatcher for a lesser role for government in the economy. In dealing with the more complex issues of his time, he was the Great Simplifier. If we could get rid of some of those trees we could reduce smog in Los Angeles; if we could get the welfare queens with their Cadillacs off the welfare rolls, we could balance the budget; and if we could end the threat of nuclear devastation with Star Wars, life would be lovely. Such ideas were fatuous, but they were wonderfully simple, and they helped to give Ronald Reagan a virtually free ride on the presidency.

Kohl was the one major leader who handled the events of 1989 well enough even to gain from them, while the response of, for example, the elder George Bush bordered on irrelevance. Kohl's ideas were as simple as Reagan's but they happened to be politically important and even profound rather than silly. They were to unify Germany and to unify Europe, two of the most constructive international political moves of the latter half of the twentieth century – rivaled only by Mikhail Gorbachev's ending of the Cold War, with its desperate nuclear stand-off, and his demolition of the Soviet empire. The details involved in working out Kohl's ideas have been complicated and difficult, but what the first George Bush, in his often comic abuse of English, called "the vision thing" was clear and simple in each of these ideas. The striking thing about Kohl's success, which must be envied by leaders in other democratic nations, is that it was grounded in genuinely simple, focused ideas that deeply mattered. In this respect, he was historically lucky. Few leaders face such simplicity and clarity of purpose. Those few mostly have been in times of war and massive economic failure. Kohl had the extraordinary luck to come to face two essentially creative and positive goals and he had the political sense to grasp them.[38]

Barring such luck as Kohl had, politicians can no longer focus their campaigns on issues as simple as the economic division that served through the time of Reagan and Thatcher. Declining confidence in the capacity of elected officials to handle policies on diverse, complex issues, coupled with the failure of systematic party definitions of those issues, may push candidates for public office in essentially opposite directions. Many may attempt to strengthen their appeal by more rigidly adhering to policy commitments on well-defined issues, such as environmental issues or the issues of the social agenda of religious values in the United States. Others may follow the lead of Bill Clinton, Tony Blair, and Gerhard Schröder and avoid association with very much at all. Not merely can they rise above party; they can rise above issues. In our era of audience democracy (Manin 1997), they can campaign on almost nothing beyond personal appeal and the promise that they will serve us well no matter what the issues are.

In the United States, the next most successful politician after Reagan would have been Clinton, if he had been able to control the adolescence of his libido. His brilliant political move was to put party definition of positions in the past, to blur the old distinctions. Or maybe it was not a brilliant move but merely the product of his character. Even here, Reagan had led the way by running the largest deficits in peacetime history, contrary to his supposedly deeply held Republican convictions. If it had not been for the related rise of the social agenda and its happenstance attachment to the extreme wing of the Republican party, Clinton might have ridden through his presidency with the ease displayed by Reagan. Despite his partial disgrace, however, the seemingly deliberate lack of much systematic content in his views may still be the model for many successful politicians for the next generation.

We need not suppose that candidates will now necessarily choose one of these strategies – focusing on the social agenda or practicing generalized vagueness – but only that those who do follow these strategies will have a greater tendency to get elected. It is clearly easier to go with a social agenda focus in the amorphous, decentralized US system than in systems in which national parties are more substantially in control of the agenda and of candidates. Hence, in the latter, generalized vagueness may be the choice of national parties and successful candidates.

Concluding Remarks

In general, it appears to be difficult for citizens to judge their governments as trustworthy – at best they can judge that a government seems to be competent and that it produces apparently good outcomes (Hardin 2002b, ch. 7; Ullmann-Margalit 2004). Hence, citizens can be more or less confident in government. Although they cannot be said to trust in any strong sense of that word, as spelled out in the three standard conceptions of trust, they can develop generalized distrust in response to seeming failures (Montinola 2004). At that point, they could say that government is either incompetent or badly motivated, but they might not have evidence to decide which of these is the problem. (It would be seen as badly motivated if, for example, its policy was thought to be a response to payoffs or to special interests.) If either incompetence or bad motivation is true of some area of government regulatory effort, however, citizens can distrust the government with respect to that area. In such contexts distrust and trust are asymmetric. Mere confidence, however, may not be as sharply asymmetric because it can be based simply on evidence of how well government does its jobs without any real understanding of how it behaves within its agencies.

If government handles crises and disasters well, it can be given credit for its seeming competence even while it is held accountable for failing to prevent the crisis or disaster, in the same way as the US government received widespread praise for its handling of the al-Qaeda terrorist organization after

September 11 but has been heavily criticized for its prior failures to follow up leads that might have prevented the disastrous attacks that day and for deflecting its purpose into the Iraq quagmire. Similarly, urban citizens can do little more than react to government's failures that might set up disasters, and then react to its immediate handling of the crisis. Evidence that it has failed can often be glaring and inescapable and can lead to distrust. Lack of evidence of government failures, however, is not sufficient to conclude in favor of generalized trust in government in many regulatory areas.

A significant part of the cause of apparently declining confidence in government may simply be an expression of intolerance of ambiguity. The clarities of an earlier era are gone. People who do not like ambiguity may trick themselves into seeing political issues as clear by simply focusing on a single clear issue and neglecting the large array of other issues. Forget the impossible ghetto or immigrant community; save whales or keep the brain-dead on life support. They might still lose confidence in government because they might suppose government does not share their correct concern with issue X. Those who can handle ambiguity easily might be comfortable with ill-defined candidates and parties that may do little more than look good.

The significance of contemporary domestic political issues in the advanced democracies may be less than it once was and yet conflict over current issues may be more fractious – not necessarily more heated or deeper but merely more fractious. Oddly, the earlier problems may have been fundamentally more difficult, but it was relatively clear what the issues were.

In 1840 John Stuart Mill ([1840] 1977: 175) wrote that America had few outstanding public leaders for the enviable reason that "America needs very little government." He wrote before the Civil War, two world wars, the Great Depression, the Cold War, and the age of terrorism, when a bit of government might have been useful. But perhaps now, nearly two centuries later, his quip may begin to apply not only to America but also to other advanced democratic nations. We may begin to think of memorable public leaders not so much as people who accomplished anything for us but as people who could maintain themselves in office with great success. And we may praise them, as people do Clinton today, not for their policy accomplishments but for their talents in mastering their roles. We will lack confidence in government, but if we are lucky it will not matter that government is incompetent to handle our marginal but complex issues.

The US Constitution, as designed principally by James Madison, was intended to get in the way of government, not to enable government. Because of the federal nature of the nation it was to create, the government it was especially designed to block was state government, because the often petty state governments stood in the way of economic life and development at the end of the eighteenth century (see further, Hardin 1999c, esp. ch. 3). What Madison ideally wanted, however, has in some respects come to pass only recently with the slow dismantling of the statist regime that was put in place in the 1930s, largely to deal with the overreaching power of business. When the social agenda crowd, the mercantilist-statist right or the socialist-statist left, win control of government, a Madisonian must think that is a disaster. In Madison's view, the people need government for order but they do not need it to run their lives, as any of these groups would want it to do.

We may finally be in an era when government can be incompetent to manage many of its problems and *it does not matter* very much. It does not matter just so long as there are no massive crises to manage and the government does not go back to Hamiltonian desires for mercantilist management of industry or socialist desires for central planning. What we have done to a large extent is back down from 1930s statism in the United States, and from Bismarckian and socialist statism in Europe, and mercantilist statism in Japan.[39] The move in much of Europe and Japan may be slower than in the UK and the US and, indeed, Japan continues to be remarkably mercantilist despite the fact that Japanese firms have been extraordinarily successful in world competition and probably do not need the protections the state still enforces.

The remarkable feature of all of this intellectually is that the former statist vision seemed to be very good and even necessary. Now it seems wrong-headed. Maybe the reason for the change of view is not that we were wrong before but that conditions have changed out from under the earlier view. The economy is finally close to freestanding, as pockets of it always have been. But the freestanding pockets in the past were usually in minor industries and, often, local areas, or in innovative activities. Now it is freestanding even in standard core activities. Perhaps even more important, business no longer seems to want to control government, which, in many nations, it has learned it does not need for its own management. Hence, the weakening of government does not matter as it once would have because we do not need such strong government to stand against business tendencies to push for mercantilist advantage. In some ways, the rise of statism was an antidote to politically ruthless business and we may no longer need it. The dread of corporate power that was once commonplace (Dewey [1935] 1987) is virtually past in the advanced economies.

The nearest equivalent to Madisonian theory in the twentieth century has been Austrian economics, as represented by F. A. Hayek (1960) and others. Theirs is ostensibly an economic theory, but in fact its most cogent insights are essentially in broad social theory. An especially odd aspect of the current hegemony of Austrian and Madisonian views, even if without those labels attached, is that the Austrian and Madisonian views were almost purely theoretical – there was no way to test them on the ground. But now they have been and are being tested and they seem to be doing very well. Madison himself was not willing to practice his theory once he got in office and perhaps Hayek and others would not have been either. But the comparison of the Soviet world, admittedly a bad version of socialist statism, and the severely trammeled markets of the more prosperous West give us a chance to see a crude, perhaps second-best test of the Austrian–Madisonian views played out.

This assessment, made in medias res, might turn out to be grossly optimistic, a mere extrapolation from the most constructive parts of current changes. But for the moment, the Austrian school and Madison seem to have the right vision. That is a stunning turn, perhaps more stunning to those on the traditional left than to Millian libertarians. Its most impressive implication is the reversal of the long historical trend toward the increasing hegemony of the state over the economy and, potentially, all else when the state fell into bad hands, such as Stalin's or Hitler's. But for that very reason, the contemporary worries about declining state capacity may be a concern grounded in understandings of the past that may be irrelevant to the present and near future. Declining confidence in government may well be evidence of a trend toward the declining role of government in certain activities that it was not wise enough to handle anyway, often because incumbents could gain opportunistic short-run advantage from manipulating the economy. For the time being, Madison and the Austrians and the theory of liberal distrust may return to favor and we may welcome distrust in government.

Notes

1 Note also how late in history the term trust arose.
2 Lott praised Strom Thurmond, the segregationist from South Carolina for his correct stance in favor of social order. Lott was very soon thereafter forced to resign as majority leader in the Senate.
3 It was this election that provoked Marx's quip that history repeats itself – the first time as tragedy and the second as farce.
4 Or that the American Anti-Federalists praised at the time they opposed the adoption, in 1878, of the US constitution (see Storing 1981).
5 Montinola goes further to argue that widespread government corruption tends to lead also to lack of trust between officials within government, and distrust between citizens.
6 Aristotle says roughly the same: "There is no harmonious relationship [philia] without trust [pistis] and there is no trust without time" (*Eudemian Ethics* VII.2.1237b12–16, in Barnes 1984: 1960). I owe the translation here to Paul Bullen, personal communication, Feb. 26, 1998. Harmonious relationships include rich relationships of friendship but also strictly impersonal ones based exclusively on self-interest.
7 Although one cannot choose to trust but can only have trust happen to oneself, one could choose to act as though one trusted.
8 Sztompka rightly excludes mere expectations of how nature will treat us to focus only on expectations of how people and entities, such as organizations and goods, that are aggregates or products of people will treat us (1999: 20). Expectations of

sociological aggregates tend to edge toward expectations of natural phenomena in some contexts and the dividing line between these two categories may not be the best place to look for a definition of trust.

9 Speaking of trust as placing a bet in a risky context, Sztompka says "it is a paradox that trust itself, that is, acting 'as if' the risk was small or nonexistent, in fact adds another risk, the 'risk of trusting.' Trust copes with one type of risk by trading it off for another type of risk" (1999: 32). If trust is based on an assessment of another's trustworthiness in a relevant context, it is clearly apt to be a matter of degree; there is no assumption that the risk is nonexistent, there is merely the risk. Our degree of trust just is our assessment of the risk we face. The degree of risk we think we face in attempting a cooperative venture with you is roughly inverse to the degree to which we trust you. High risk means low trust.

10 However, Hollis argues, we still need trust for economic progress. This set of claims is similar to Fukuyama's (1995) assertions that familial trust facilitates the creation of small-scale enterprises. Unfortunately it also leads to distrust of others not in the family, and this distrust limits the likelihood of more expansive enterprises and the extent of economic growth.

11 An early positivist might say the measure is the concept. Wright and Tedeschi (1975) separate Rotter's scale into three factors: paternal trust, political trust, and trust of strangers. Hence, degrees of trust vary by the object of the trust, as we all must know from our own stances.

12 Hence, generalized cynicism can make sense just as generalized distrust can make sense (as will be argued in chapter 6).

13 Over the years, researchers have used other labels to describe what the NES trust questions measure, including political cynicism, disaffection, and alienation (see Citrin and Muste 1999). The items in the GSS might also be useful for tapping cynicism. For further discussion see Cook, Hardin, and Levi 2005, ch. 1.

14 It seems reasonable to assume, with David Hume ([1742] 1985a), that many government officials are no more public-spirited than most citizens and that by far most of the success government has in achieving public purposes turns on the structures of incentives that guide individual officials in their actions (Hardin 1998a). Hence, it is unlikely that the public-spiritedness of officials has markedly declined.

15 Niklas Luhmann (1980) speaks somewhat loosely of *system* trust, which is merely the confidence one has in the larger system of legal enforcement, monetary policy, and so forth, and is therefore not trust in any useful sense anymore than my expectation that drivers will stay to the right is a matter of trusting them to have my specific interests at heart.

16 These reasons fit the encapsulated interest conception of trust.

17 One cannot sensibly be thought to have a moral commitment to fulfill trusts tout court. If I did, and you happened to trust me to do something I would and should never do, then the fact that you trusted me to do so would morally bind me to some extent. Nevertheless, some writers actually suppose one is morally obligated to fulfill trusts in oneself.

18 James Coleman attributes the term to Glenn Loury (1977, 1987). But it was used even earlier in roughly the relevant sense by Jane Jacobs (1961: 138) and Lyda Judson Hanifan (1916). See Ostrom and Ahn (2003) for the history and development of the idea of social capital.

19 This is not impossible. There might be feedback from trust to more trust. This is, however, not the apparent claim of Putnam and others

20 The supposition that the production of relevant forms of human capital – forms that might be especially important in our political lives – is being increasingly handled through the experiences of our professional lives in organizations may be false. It may be that we are actually increasingly in deficit, relative to earlier generations, in developing such politically relevant human capital. This will not be an easily resolved empirical question.

21 Becker's (1996) social capital is from social effects on one's tastes and the utility one gets from various consumptions. For example, my social capital might include my capacity for gaining great pleasure from music of a particular kind or my incapacity to enjoy some food that comes under a taboo in my social group. More generally, the social influences of my peers, community, or reference group on my tastes – and therefore on my utility from various consumptions – are instances of my social capital in Becker's sense. What I have directly experienced that has affected my tastes for some consumption goods is an instance of Becker's personal capital. Becker's concern is quite different from that of the other analysts of social capital, and it will not be discussed extensively here.

22 The incentive might be trumped by other considerations, so that even the best of trusting relationships can fail when the stakes get high.

23 There is a commonplace claim that trust will beget trustworthiness (see contributions to Braithwaite and Levi 1998). Schotter and Sopher (2006) do not find this to be true in game experiments that they run, while they do find that trustworthiness (cooperativeness in the play of games) does beget trust (or cooperation). In any case, the claim that trust begets trustworthiness is generally misstated by its proponents. They generally mean that acting as though one does trust will lead others to become trustworthy.

24 This comment is made in a brief discussion of the large body of recent work on irrational aspects of choice behavior. Much of this work focuses on anomalies and gives sly and sometimes cute explanations of them.

25 Kafka (1967, entry for Oct. 17, 1921) held the idea of marriage to be beautiful, but he doubted that any instance of it was very good.

26 If one uses anything from a hobbyist's website, verification can be a major issue. Websites and online message boards recently have defended Kobe Bryant against sexual assault charges with extraordinary venom directed at the woman making the charge and everyone associated with her. It is exceedingly unlikely that these internet-assisted libelers have any knowledge on which to base their claims. They have only energy and partisan commitments. Getting caught up in the thrall of a sports fan evidently reduces a person's IQ by approximately 23 points. Because news networks and television stations want their own websites to have many hits, they put in links to the irresponsible sites. CBS, for example, could get thousands of hits while keeping itself formally out of the libelous debate, which it merely enabled others to enter with greater ease (Roberts 2003).

27 The network is at www.orgnet.com/leftright.html. An updated 2004 network pattern is at www.orgnet.com/divided.html.

28 One of the most remarkable cases of adopting an identity is John Howard Griffin ([1960] 2004) who had himself blackened so that he could travel the South in the United States in 1959 in order to experience the life of racial discrimination.

29 Such romantic involvements might be risky in ways that only the internet can threaten. Several years ago, one of the Stanford University servers was reported to have randomly re-addressed emails of people with last names beginning with the first three letters of the alphabet. The possibilities range from the disastrous to the hilarious. Boastful emails about affairs have been resent to thousands of people, have made it into the

international press, and have repaid the boasters with grim repercussions, including lost jobs.

30 It also encourages a perverse form of inefficient brevity, as when someone sends a quick reply and then follows it almost immediately with several additional notes to cover neglected points.

31 This discussion draws on Hardin 2002b.

32 This is the Commerce Clause, US Constitution, Article 3, section 8: "The Congress shall have Power . . . To regulate Commerce with foreign Nations, and among the several States, and with the Indian Tribes."

33 In Texas, seats were re-districted to knock Democrats out of office and to create slight majority districts favoring Republicans while putting the large majority of all Democratic voters into a small number of districts. This resulted in a shift of six seats, or more than the three incumbents who lost in all other races.

34 Results for 2002 were similar (Richie 2002).

35 Those debates may also have elevated misunderstanding to new heights. For example, many of the French electorate apparently thought they were voting on policies that are determined by the World Trade Organization (WTO), not the EU.

36 One might make a strong case for William Howard Taft.

37 Their intervention turned out not to be necessary when the courts ruled that forcing the parties into open primaries unconstitutionally violated their freedom of association. For further referendums often gone awry, see Gerber et al. 2001.

38 Unfortunately for his long-term reputation, he did not have the political sense to avoid corruption.

39 Outside the advanced democracies, many other nations have also backed down from socialist-communist statism, both in the former Communist bloc and in the Third World (except for the Arab-Islamic world, which is almost everywhere still mired in statist control of economic and social policy, typically under the control of men utterly ignorant of any social or economic theory or even devoid of ideas entirely). The development of the Third World now appears, retrospectively, to have been massively hampered by its adherence, roughly, to socialist-statism. For example, Jawaharlal Nehru's autarkic statism doomed two generations of Indians to at best halting progress in overcoming massive poverty and illiteracy.

References

Adams, John [1787] 1987. "Defense of Constitutions of Government of the United States." In vol. 1 of Philip Kurland and Ralph Lerner (eds), *The Founders' Constitution*, 5 vols, Chicago: University of Chicago Press, pp. 59–60.

Addario, Lynsey 2001. "Jihad's Women." *New York Times Magazine*, Oct. 21, pp. 38–41.

Ahn, T. K., Elinor Ostrom, David Schmidt, and James Walker 2002. "Trust in Two-Person Games: Game Structures and Linkages." In Elinor Ostrom and Jimmy Walker (eds), *Trust and Reciprocity*, New York: Russell Sage Foundation.

Akerlof, George 1970. "The Market for 'Lemons': Qualitative Uncertainty and the Market Mechanism," *Quarterly Journal of Economics* 84: 488–500.

Alba, Richard D., and Victor Nee 2003. *Remaking the American Mainstream: Assimilation and Contemporary Immigration*. Cambridge: Harvard University Press.

Allen, James, Hilton Als, John Lewis, and Leon F. Litwack 2000. *Without Sanctuary: Lynching Photography in America*. Santa Fe: Twin Palms.

Almond, Gabriel, and Sidney Verba 1965. *The Civic Culture*. Boston: Little, Brown.

Alstyne, Marshall Van, and Erik Brynjolsson 1996. "Could the Internet Balkanize Science?" *Science*, Nov. 29, pp. 1479–80.

Anderson, Scott 2003. "The Makeover." *New York Times Magazine*, Jan. 19, pp. 28ff.

"The Anonymous Iamblichi" 1995. In Michael Gagarin and Paul Woodruff (eds), *Early Greek Political Thought from*

Homer to the Sophists, Cambridge: Cambridge University Press, pp. 290–5.

Arrow, Kenneth J. [1951] 1963. *Social Choice and Individual Values*, 2nd edn. New Haven: Yale University Press.

——1974. *The Limits of Organization*. New York: W. W. Norton.

Banfield, Edward C. 1958. *The Moral Basis of a Backward Society*. New York: Free Press.

Barber, Bernard 1983. *The Logic and Limits of Trust*. New Brunswick: Rutgers University Press.

Barnes, Jonathan (ed.) 1984. *The Collected Works of Aristotle*. Princeton: Princeton University Press.

Beck, Ulrich 1992. *Risk Society*. London: Sage.

Becker, Gary S. [1957] 1971. *The Economics of Discrimination*, 2nd edn. Chicago: University of Chicago Press.

——[1964] 1975. *Human Capital: A Theoretical and Empirical Analysis, with Special Reference to Education*, 2nd edn. New York: Columbia University Press.

——1996. *Accounting for Tastes*. Cambridge: Harvard University Press.

Beer, Samuel H. 1993. *To Make a Nation: The Rediscovery of American Federalism*. Cambridge: Harvard University Press.

Bianco, William 1994. *Trust: Representatives and Constituents*. Ann Arbor: University of Michigan Press.

Bimber, Bruce A., and Richard Davis 2003. *Campaigning Online: The Internet in US Elections*. New York: Oxford University Press.

Bohnet, Iris, and Richard Zeckhauser 2004. "Trust, Risk, and Betrayal." *Journal of Economic Behavior and Organization* 55 (4): 467–84.

Bolton, Gary E., Elena Katok, and Axel Ockenfels 2004. "Trust among Internet Traders." *Analyse und Kritik* (Dec.): 185–202.

Boyer, Peter J. 1995. "Children of Waco." *New Yorker*, Apr. 15, pp. 38–45.

Braithwaite, Valerie, and Margaret Levi (eds) 1998. *Trust and Governance*. New York: Russell Sage Foundation.

Brehm, John, and Wendy Rahn 1997. "Individual-Level Evidence for the Causes and Consequences of Social Capital." *American Journal of Political Science* 41: 999–1023.

Byrne, Muriel St Clare (ed.) 1983. *The Lisle Letters: An Abridgement*. Chicago: University of Chicago Press.

Citrin, Jack, and Christopher Muste 1999. "Trust in Government and System Support." In J. Robinson, L. Wrightsman, and P. Shaver (eds), *Measures of Political Attitudes*, New York: Academic Press, pp. 465–532.

Coleman, James S. 1988. "Social Capital in the Creation of Human Capital." *American Journal of Sociology* (Supplement) 94: S95–120.

——1991. *Foundations of Social Theory*. Cambridge: Harvard University Press.

Cook, Karen S., and Robin M. Cooper 2003. "Experimental Studies of Cooperation, Trust and Social Exchange." In Elinor Ostrom and James Walker (eds), *Trust and Reciprocity: Interdisciplinary Lessons for Experimental Research*, New York: Russell Sage Foundation, pp. 209–44.

Cook, Karen S., and Richard M. Emerson 1978. "Power, Equity and Commitment in Exchange Networks." *American Sociological Review* 43 (5): 721–39.

Cook, Karen S., and Russell Hardin 2001. "Norms of Cooperativeness and Networks of Trust." In Michael Hechter and Karl-Dieter Opp (eds), *Social Norms*, New York: Russell Sage Foundation, pp. 327–47.

Cook, Karen S., Russell Hardin, and Margaret Levi 2005. *Cooperation without Trust?* New York: Russell Sage Foundation.

Coye, Cheshire, and Karen S. Cook 2004. "The Emergence of Trust Networks under Uncertainty: Implications for Internet Interactions." *Analyse und Kritik* (Dec.): 220–41.

Crossette, Barbara 2001. "Living in a World without Women," *New York Times*, Nov. 4, sec. 4:1.

Dahl, Robert A. 1971. *Polyarchy*. New Haven: Yale University Press.

Dalton, Russell J., Susan J. Pharr, and Robert D. Putnam 2000. "A Quarter Century of Declining Confidence." *Journal of Democracy* 11 (Apr.): 5–25.

Dasgupta, Partha 1988. "Trust as a Commodity." In Diego Gambetta (ed.), *Trust: Making and Breaking Cooperative Relations*, Oxford: Blackwell, pp. 49–72.

de Waal, Frans B. M. 2003. "The Chimpanzee's Service Economy: Evidence for Cognition-Based Reciprocal Exchange." In Elinor Ostrom and James Walker (eds), *Trust and Reciprocity: Interdisciplinary Lessons from Experimental Research*, New York: Russell Sage, pp. 128–43.

Dewey, John [1935] 1987. *Liberalism and Social Action*. In vol. 11 of *The Later Works of Dewey, 1925–1953*, Carbondale: Southern Illinois University Press.

Diamond, Jared M. 2005. *Collapse: How Societies Choose to Fail or Succeed*. New York: Viking.

Downs, Anthony 1957. *An Economic Theory of Democracy*. New York: Harper.

Dray, Philip 2002. *At the Hands of Persons Unknown: The Lynching of Black America*. New York: Random House.

Durkheim, Émile [1893] 1933. *The Division of Labor in Society*. New York: Macmillan.

Dworkin, Ronald 2000. *Sovereign Virtue: The Theory and Practice of Equality*. Cambridge: Harvard University Press.

Eckel, Catherine C., and Rick K. Wilson 2004. "Is Trust a Risky Decision?" *Journal of Economic Behavior and Organization* 55 (4): 447–65.

Emerson, Richard 1962. "Power-Dependence Relations." *American Sociological Review* 27 (1): 31–41.

——1964. "Power-Dependence Relations: Two Experiments." *Sociometry* 27 (3): 282–98.

Estrich, Susan 1998. *Getting Away with Murder: How Politics is Destroying the Criminal Justice System*. Cambridge: Harvard University Press.

Etzioni, Amitai 1993. *The Spirit of Community: Rights, Responsibilities, and the Communitarian Agenda*. New York: Crown.

Etzioni, Amitai, and Thomas A. Diprete 1979. "The Decline in Confidence in America: The Prime Factor, a Research Note." *Journal of Applied Behavioral Science* 15 (Nov.–Dec.): 520–6.

Farrell, Henry 2004. "Trust, Distrust, and Power in Inter-firm Relations." In Russell Hardin (ed.), *Distrust*, New York: Russell Sage Foundation.

Fehr, Ernst, Urs Fischbacher, Bernhard von Rosenbladt, Jürgen Schupp, and Gert G. Wagner 2002. "A Nation-Wide Laboratory: Examining Trust and Trustworthiness by Integrating Behavioral Experiments into Representative Surveys." *Schmollers Jahrbuch* 122 (4): 519–42.

Fischer, Claude S. 1982. *To Dwell among Friends: Personal Networks in Town and City*. Chicago: University of Chicago Press.

Flexner, Abraham 1910. *Medical Education in the United States and Canada: A Report to the Carnegie Foundation for the Advancement of Teaching with an Introduction by Henry Pritchett*. Bulletin no. 4. New York: Carnegie Foundation for the Advancement of Teaching.

Fukuyama, Francis 1995. *Trust: The Social Virtues and the Creation of Prosperity*. New York: Free Press.

Gambetta, Diego (ed.) 1988. *Trust: Making and Breaking Cooperative Relations*. Oxford: Blackwell.

Gamson, William A. 1968. *Power and Discontent*. Homewood, IL: Dorsey.

Gerber, Elisabeth R., Arthur Lupia, Mathew D. McCubbins, and D. Roderick Kiewiet 2001. *Stealing the Initiative: How State*

Government Responds to Direct Democracy. Upper Saddle River, NJ: Prentice Hall.

Gibson, James L. 2001. "Social Networks, Civil Society, and the Prospects for Consolidating Russia's Democratic Transition." *American Journal of Political Science* 45: 51–69.

Giddens, Anthony 1990. *The Consequences of Modernity*. Cambridge: Polity.

Glaeser, Edward L., David I. Laibson, José A. Scheinkman, and Christine L. Soutter 2000. "Measuring Trust." *Quarterly Journal of Economics* 115 (Aug.): 811–46.

Goldthorpe, John H., David Lockwood, Frank Bechhofer, and Jennifer Platt 1969. *The Affluent Worker in the Class Structure*. Cambridge: Cambridge University Press.

Griffin, John Howard [1960] 2004. *Black Like Me*. San Antonio: Wings Press.

Güth, Werner, and Hartmut Kliemt 2004. "The Evolution of Trust(worthiness) in the Net." *Analyse und Kritik* (Dec.): 203–19.

Gutmann, Amy, and Dennis Thompson 2004. *Why Deliberative Democracy?* Princeton: Princeton University Press.

Hafner, Katie 2004. "With Internet Fraud Up Sharply, Ebay Attracts Vigilantes." *New York Times*, Mar. 20, A1 and C2.

Hamilton, Alexander, John Jay, and James Madison. [1787] 2001. *The Federalist Papers*, ed. George W. Carey and James McClellan, the Gideon edition. Indianapolis: Liberty Fund.

Hanifan, Lyda J. 1916. "The Rural School Community Center." *Annals of the American Academy of Political and Social Science* 67: 130–8.

Hardin, Russell 1982a. *Collective Action*. Baltimore: Johns Hopkins University Press for Resources for the Future.

——— 1982b. "Exchange Theory on Strategic Bases." *Social Science Information* 21 (2): 251–72.

——— 1987. "Rational Choice Theories." In Terence Ball (ed.), *Idioms of Inquiry: Critique and Renewal in Political Science*, Albany: SUNY Press, pp. 67–91.

——— 1988. *Morality within the Limits of Reason*. Chicago: University of Chicago Press.

——— 1991. "Trusting Persons, Trusting Institutions." In Richard J. Zeckhauser (ed.), *The Strategy of Choice*, Cambridge: MIT Press, pp. 185–209.

——— 1992. "The Street-Level Epistemology of Trust." *Analyse und Kritik* 14 (Dec.): 152–76 (repr. in *Politics and Society* 21 (Dec.) (1993): 505–29).

——— 1995. *One for All: The Logic of Group Conflict*. Princeton: Princeton University Press.

—— 1996. "Trustworthiness." *Ethics* 107 (Oct.): 26–42.

—— 1997. "The Economics of Religious Belief." *Journal of Institutional and Theoretical Economics* 153: 259–78.

—— 1998a. "Institutional Commitment: Values or Incentives?" In Avner Ben Ner and Louis Putterman (eds), *Economics, Values, and Organization*, Cambridge: Cambridge University Press, pp. 419–33.

—— 1998b. "Trust in Government." In Valerie Braithwaite and Margaret Levi (eds), *Trust and Governance*, New York: Russell Sage Foundation, pp. 9–27.

—— 1999a. "From Bodo Ethics to Distributive Justice." *Ethical Theory and Moral Practice* 2 (4): 337–63.

—— 1999b. "Social Capital." In James Alt, Margaret Levi, and Elinor Ostrom (eds), *Competition and Cooperation: Conversations with Nobelists about Economics and Political Science*, New York: Russell Sage Foundation, pp. 170–89.

—— 1999c. *Liberalism, Constitutionalism, and Democracy.* Oxford: Oxford University Press.

—— 2000. "Democratic Epistemology and Accountability." *Social Philosophy and Policy* 17: 110–26.

—— 2001. "The Crippled Epistemology of Extremism." In Albert Breton, Gianluigi Galeotti, Pierre Salmon, and Ronald Wintrobe (eds), *Political Extremism and Rationality*, Cambridge: Cambridge University Press.

—— 2002a. "The Street-Level Epistemology of Democratic Participation." *Journal of Political Philosophy* 10 (2): 212–29 (repr. in vol. 7 of James Fishkin and Peter Laslett (eds), *Philosophy, Politics and Society*, Oxford: Blackwell, 2003, pp. 163–81).

—— 2002b. *Trust and Trustworthiness.* New York: Russell Sage Foundation.

—— 2003. *Indeterminacy and Society.* Princeton: Princeton University Press.

Harrington, James 1656. *The Common-Wealth of Oceana.* London.

Hayek, F. A. 1960. *The Constitution of Liberty.* Chicago: University of Chicago Press.

Heimer, Carol 1990. "Comment [on Hardin]." In Karen Cook and Margaret Levi (eds), *The Limits of Rationality*, Chicago: University of Chicago Press, pp. 378–82.

Hertzberg, Lars 1988. "On the Attitude of Trust." *Inquiry* 31: 307–22.

Hibbing, John R., and Elizabeth Theiss-Morse 2002. *Stealth Democracy: Americans' Beliefs about How Government Should Work.* Cambridge: Cambridge University Press.

Hindman, Matthew 2004. "The Real Lessons of Howard Dean: Reflections on the First Digital Campaign." *Perspectives on Politics* 3 (Mar.): 121–8.

Hirschman, Albert O. 1982. *Shifting Involvements: Private Interest and Public Action.* Princeton: Princeton University Press.

Hobbes, Thomas [1651] 1994. *Leviathan*, ed. Edwin Curley. Indianapolis: Hackett.

Hollis, Martin 1998. *Trust within Reason.* Cambridge: Cambridge University Press.

Hume, David [1739–40] 1978. *A Treatise of Human Nature*, ed. L. A. Selby-Bigge and P. H. Nidditch, 2nd edn. Oxford: Oxford University Press.

——[1742] 1985. "Of the Independency of Parliament." In *David Hume: Essays Moral, Political, and Literary*, ed. Eugene F. Miller, Indianapolis: Liberty Classics, pp. 42–6.

——[1751] 1975. *An Enquiry Concerning the Principles of Morals.* In Hume, *Enquiries*, ed. L. A. Selby-Bigge and P. H. Nidditch, 3rd edn, Oxford: Oxford University Press, pp. 167–323,

——[1752] 1985. "Idea of a Perfect Commonwealth." In *David Hume: Essays Moral, Political, and Literary*, ed. Eugene F. Miller, Indianapolis: Liberty Classics, pp. 512–29.

Jacobs, Jane 1961. *The Death and Life of Great American Cities.* New York: Random House.

James, Harvey S., Jr. 2002. "On the Reliability of Trusting." *Rationality and Society* 14 (2): 229–56.

Kafka, Franz 1967. *Tagebücher* (Diaries). Frankfurt: Fischer.

Kawabata, Yasunari 1974. *The Lake*, trans. Reiko Tsukimura. Tokyo: Kodansha.

King, Anthony 2000. "Distrust of Government: Explaining American Exceptionalism." In Susan J. Pharr and Robert D. Putnam (eds), *Disaffected Democracies: What's Troubling the Trilateral Democracies*, Princeton: Princeton University Press, pp. 74–98.

Klein, Daniel B. 1994. "If Government Is So Villainous, How Come Government Officials Don't Seem Like Villains?" *Economics and Philosophy* 10: 91–106.

Klitzman, Robert, and Ronald Bayer 2003. *Mortal Secrets: Truth and Lies in the Age of AIDS.* Baltimore: Johns Hopkins University Press.

Kollock, Peter 1999. "The Economics of Online Cooperation: Gifts and Public Goods in Cyberspace." In Marc A. Smith and Peter Kollock (eds), *Communities in Cyberspace*, London: Routledge, pp. 220–39.

Komito, Lee 1998. "The Net as a Foraging Society: Flexible Communities." *Information Society* 14: 97–106.

Kramer, Roderick M. 1994. "The Sinister Attribution Error: Paranoid Cognition and Collective Distrust in Organizations." *Motivation and Emotion* 18 (2): 199–230.

——1998. "Paranoid Cognition in Social Systems: Thinking and Acting in the Shadow of Doubt." *Personality and Social Psychology Review* 2: 251–75.

Kurland, Philip, and Ralph Lerner (eds) 1987. *The Founders' Constitution*. 5 vols, Chicago: University of Chicago Press.

Kurzban, Robert 2003. "Biological Foundations of Reciprocity." In Elinor Ostrom and James Walker (eds), *Trust and Reciprocity: Interdisciplinary Lessons from Experimental Research*, New York: Russell Sage, pp. 105–27.

Ladd, Everett C. 1996. "The Data Just Don't Show Erosion of America's 'Social Capital.'" *Public Perspective* (June–July): 1–22.

Leeuw, Frans L. 1997. "Solidarity between Public Sector Organizations: The Problem of Social Cohesion in the Asymmetric Society." *Rationality and Society* 9 (Nov.): 469–88.

Leijonhufvud, Axel 1995. "The Individual, the Market and the Industrial Division of Labor." In Carlo Mongardini (ed.), *L'Individuo e il mercato*, Rome: Bulzoi, pp. 61–78.

Levi, Margaret 1997. *Consent, Dissent and Patriotism*. New York: Cambridge University Press.

Lin, Ann Chih 2000. *Reform in the Making: The Implementation of Social Policy in Prison*. Princeton: Princeton University Press.

Locke, John [1690] 1988. *Two Treatises of Government*. Cambridge: Cambridge University Press.

Loury, Glenn C. 1977. "A Dynamic Theory of Racial Income Differences," In P. A. Wallace and A. Le Mund (eds), *Women, Minorities, and Employment Discrimination*, Lexington: Lexington Books, ch. 8.

——1987. "Why Should We Care about Group Inequality?" *Social Philosophy and Policy* 5: 249–71.

Luhmann, Niklas 1980. "Trust: A Mechanism for the Reduction of Social Complexity." In Luhmann, *Trust and Power*, New York: Wiley, pp. 4–103.

Macauley, Stewart 1963. "Non-contractual Relations in Business: A Preliminary Study." *American Sociological Review* 28 (Feb.): 55–67.

Macneil, Ian R. 1980. *The New Social Contract: An Inquiry into Modern Contractual Relations*. New Haven: Yale University Press.

Manin, Bernard 1997. *The Principles of Representative Government*. Cambridge: Cambridge University Press.

Marx, Karl [1852] 1963. *The 18th Brumaire of Louis Bonaparte*. New York: International.

Massing, Michael 1998. "The Blue Revolution." *New York Review of Books*, Nov. 19, pp. 32–6.

Matzat, Uwe 2004. "Cooperation and Community on the Internet: Past Issues and Present Perspectives for Theoretical-Empirical Internet Research." *Analyse und Kritik* (Dec.): 63–90.

McCabe, Kevin, and Vernon Smith 2002. "Strategic Analysis by Players in Games: What Information Do They Use?" In Elinor Ostrom and Jimmy Walker (eds), *Trust and Reciprocity*, New York: Russell Sage Foundation.

McKenna, Katelyn Y. A., and Amie S. Green 2002. "Virtual Group Dynamics." *Group Dynamics: Theory, Research and Practice* 6 (1): 116–27.

McMurtry, Larry 2000. "Hometown America's Black Book," *New York Review of Books*, Dec. 21, pp. 28–30.

Mill, John Stuart [1840] 1977. "De Tocqueville on Democracy in America, II." In vol. 18 of *Collected Works of John Stuart Mill*, ed. J. M. Robson, Toronto: University of Toronto Press, pp. 153–204.

——[1861] 1977. *Considerations on Representative Government.* In Mill, *Essays on Politics and Society*, vol. 19 of *Collected Works of John Stuart Mill*, ed. J. M. Robson, Toronto: University of Toronto Press, pp. 371–613.

Montesquieu, Charles le Secondat, Baron de [1748] 1989. *The Spirit of the Laws.* Cambridge: Cambridge University Press.

Montinola, Gabriella 2004. "Corruption, Distrust, and the Deterioration of the Rule of Law." In Russell Hardin (ed.), *Distrust*, New York: Russell Sage Foundation: 298–323.

Mueller, John 1999. *Democracy, Capitalism, and Ralph's Pretty Good Grocery.* Princeton: Princeton University Press.

Neuman, W. R. 1986. *The Paradox of Mass Politics: Knowledge and Opinion in the American Electorate.* Cambridge: Harvard University Press.

Neumann, John von, and Oskar Morgenstern [1944] 1953. *Theory of Games and Economic Behavior*, 3rd edn. Princeton: Princeton University Press.

Newton, Kenneth, and Pippa Norris 2000. "Confidence in Public Institutions: Faith, Culture or Performance." In Susan J. Pharr and Robert Putnam (eds), *Disaffected Democracies*, Princeton: Princeton University Press, pp. 52–73.

Ostrom, Elinor 2002. "Towards a Behavioral Theory Linking Reciprocity, Reputation, and Trust." In Elinor Ostrom and Jimmy Walker (eds), *Trust and Reciprocity*, New York: Russell Sage Foundation.

Ostrom, Elinor, and T. K. Ahn (eds) 2003. *Foundations of Social Capital.* Cheltenham: Elgar.

Ostrom, Elinor, and Jimmy Walker (eds) 2002. *Trust and Reciprocity*. New York: Russell Sage Foundation.

Parry, Geraint 1976. "Trust, Distrust, and Consensus." *British Journal of Political Science* 6: 129–42.

Parsons, Talcott [1937] 1968. *The Structure of Social Action*. New York: Free Press.

Patterson, Orlando 1999. "Liberty against the Democratic State: On the Historical and Contemporary Sources of American Distrust." In Mark Warren (ed.), *Democracy and Trust*, Cambridge: Cambridge University Press, pp. 151–207.

Pharr, Susan J., and Robert D. Putnam (eds) 2000. *Disaffected Democracies: What's Troubling the Trilateral Democracies*. Princeton: Princeton University Press.

Portes, Alejandro, and Patricia Landolt 1996. "The Downside of Social Capital." *American Prospect* 26: 18–22.

Portes, Alejandro, and Julia Sensenbrenner 1993. "Embeddedness and Immigration: Notes on the Social Determinants of Economic Action," *American Journal of Sociology* 98: 1320–50.

Putnam, Robert D. 1993. *Making Democracy Work: Civic Traditions in Modern Italy*. Princeton: Princeton University Press.

——1995a. "Tuning In, Tuning Out: The Strange Disappearance of Social Capital in America," *PS: Political Science and Politics* 28 (4): 664–83.

——1995b. "Bowling Alone: America's Declining Social Capital." *Journal of Democracy* 6: 65–78.

——2000. *Bowling Alone: The Collapse and Revival of American Community*. New York: Simon and Schuster.

Rapoport, Anatol, and Albert M. Chammah 1965. *Prisoner's Dilemma*. Ann Arbor: University of Michigan Press.

Richie, Rob 2002. "Fair Elections Update: Election 2002 and the Case for Reform." Center for Voting and Democracy, Washington, Nov. 14.

Riesenberg, Peter 1992. *Citizenship in the Western Tradition: From Plato to Rousseau*. Chapel Hill: University of North Carolina Press.

Roberts, Selena. 2003. "A Feeding Frenzy on the Web Shoves Sanity Right out the Door." *New York Times*, July 27, sec. 8, p. 6.

Rose, Richard 1994. "Postcommunism and the Problem of Trust." *Journal of Democracy* 5 (3):18–30.

Rotter, Julian B. 1967. "A New Scale for the Measurement of Interpersonal Trust." *Journal of Personality* 35 (4): 651–65.

——1971. "Generalized Expectancies for Interpersonal Trust." *American Psychologist* 26 (5): 443–50.

——1980. "Interpersonal Trust, Trustworthiness, and Gullibility," *American Psychologist* 35: 1–7.

Sajo, Andras 1999. *Limited Government: An Introduction to Constitutionalism*. Budapest: Central European University Press.

Schelling, Thomas C. 1960. *The Strategy of Conflict*. Cambridge: Harvard University Press.

Schotter, Andrew, and Barry Sopher 2006. "Trust and Trustworthiness in Games: An Experimental Study of Intergenerational Advice." *Experimental Economics*, forthcoming.

Schultz, Theodore W. 1963. *The Economic Value of Education*. New York: Columbia University Press.

Schumpeter, Joseph A. [1942] 1950. *Capitalism, Socialism and Democracy*, 3rd edn. New York: Harper.

Seligman, Adam B. 1997. *The Problem of Trust*. Princeton: Princeton University Press.

Sen, Amartya 1982. "Equality of What?" In Sen, *Choice, Welfare and Measurement*, Cambridge: MIT Press, pp. 353–69.

Skeat, Walter W. [1879–82] 1910. *An Etymological Dictionary of the English Language*, 4th edn. Oxford: Oxford University Press.

Skocpol, Theda 2003. *Diminished Democracy: From Membership to Management in American Civic Life*. Norman: Oklahoma University Press.

Smith, Adam [1776] 1976. *An Inquiry into the Nature and Causes of the Wealth of Nations*, ed. R. H. Campbell, A. S. Skinner, and W. B. Todd. Oxford: Oxford University Press (repr. by Liberty Press, 1979).

Snijders, Chris, and Richard Zijdeman 2004. "Reputation and Internet Auctions: eBay and Beyond." *Analyse und Kritik* (Dec.): 158–84.

Storing, Herbert J. (ed.) 1981. *The Complete Anti-Federalist*. 7 vols, Chicago: University of Chicago Press.

Sztompka, Piotr 1999. *Trust: A Sociological Theory*. Cambridge: Cambridge University Press.

Tierney, John 2004. "The Hawks Loudly Express their Second Thoughts," *New York Times*, May 16, sec. 4, p. 5.

Tocqueville, Alexis de [1835 and 1840] 1966. *Democracy in America*, trans. George Lawrence. New York: Harper and Row.

Turkle, Sherry 1996. "Who Am We?" *Wired* (4.01, Jan.), at www.wired.com/wired/archive/4.01/turkle_pr.html.

Ullmann-Margalit, Edna 2004. "Trust, Distrust, and In Between." In Russell Hardin (ed.), *Distrust*, New York: Russell Sage Foundation, pp. 60–82.

Uslaner, Eric M. 2002. *The Moral Foundations of Trust*. Cambridge: Cambridge University Press.

Wall, Helena M. 1990. *Fierce Communion: Family and Community in Early America.* Cambridge: Harvard University Press.

Warren, Mark E. 1999. "Democratic Theory and Trust." In Warren (ed.), *Democracy and Trust*, Cambridge: Cambridge University Press, pp. 310–45.

Watters, Ethan 2003. *Urban Tribes: A Generation Redefines Friendship, Family, and Commitment.* New York: Bloomsbury.

Williamson, Oliver E. 1975. *Markets and Hierarchies: Analysis and Antitrust Implications.* New York: Free Press.

—— 1981. "The Economics of Organization: The Transaction Cost Approach," *American Journal of Sociology* 87: 548–77.

—— 1985. *The Economic Institutions of Capitalism: Firms, Markets, Relational Contracting.* New York: Free Press.

Wisconsin v. Yoder et al., 406 US 205 (1972), pp. 205–49.

Wright, Thomas L., and Richard G. Tedeschi 1975. "Factor Analysis of the Interpersonal Trust Scale." *Journal of Consulting and Clinical Psychology* 43 (4): 470–7.

Yamagishi, Toshio, and Karen S. Cook 1993. "Generalized Exchange and Social Dilemmas." *Social Psychology Quarterly* 56: 235–48.

Yamagishi, Toshio, and Riki Kakiuchi 2000. "It Takes Venturing into a Tiger's Cave to Steal a Baby Tiger: Experiments on the Development of Trust Relationships." In Werner Raub and Jeroen Weesie (eds), *The Management of Durable Relations*, Amsterdam: Thela Thesis.

Yamagishi, Toshio, Masako Kikuchi, and Motoko Kosugi 1999. "Trust, Gullibility, and Social Intelligence." *Asian Journal of Social Psychology* 2 (1): 145–61.

Index

acquiescence, 69, 167
Acton, H. B., 40
Adams, John, 138, 142
al-Qaeda, 122, 175
Alien and Sedition Acts, 142
Almond, Gabriel, 158
Amazon.com, 102, 105, 108
American exceptionalism, 149
American Medical Association, 163
Amin, Idi, 143
Amish, 121–2, 132
Anti-Federalists, US, 143, 145–6, 154, 193
Argentine federation, 146
Aristotle, 193
Arrow, Kenneth, 85
Articles of Confederation, US, 136, 143
asymmetry of trust and distrust, 18, 23, 160
Austrian economics, 178

Banfield, Edward, 10
Barnes&Noble.com, 108
Bayes, Thomas, 85
Becker, Gary, 85–6, 96, 125

Becker–Coleman seminar, 87
Beer, Samuel, 144
Belgian quasi-federation, 146
Bill of Rights, US, 140
bin Laden, Osama, 133
Blair, Tony, 149, 166, 174
Bodo, 6–10
    morality of, 7
    small community of, 13, 62
    and strangers, 10
Brehm, John, 76
Bryan, William Jennings, 162–3, 171
Bush, President George H. W., 173
Bush, President George W., 30, 155, 162–3

Canada
    Amish in, 121
    and declining confidence, 1, 62, 157
capital, 85–8
    to enable trust, 89
    financial, 86, 88
    human, 76, 81–3, 86–8, 92–3, 116

capital (*cont'd*)
  institutional, 77, 88, 91,
    94–6
  internet, 99, 116
  interpersonal, 79, 84, 87–91,
    94–6
  network, 79–81, 92, 99
  organizational, 79, 81, 83,
    92–3, 99
  physical, 86, 88
  see also social capital
central planning, 63, 66, 165,
  177
civic generation, 5
civic mindedness, 5, 12
civil liberties
  and terrorism, 118–19, 129,
    130–1, 133
  in US law, 130
Civil War, English, 140
Civil War, US, 163
class consciousness, 9
Clinton, Bill, 167, 172, 174,
  177
cognition, paranoid, 113–15
cognitive, trust as, 17, 27, 33,
  38, 56, 96
Cold War, 173
Coleman, James S., 44–5,
  76–9, 86–7, 95
collective action, 43, 76
Commerce Clause (US
  Constitution), 135, 141,
  150
communitarianism, 12–13, 97,
  123, 143, 161
  negative implications of, 123
communities, small, 5, 6, 13,
  14, 128
competence
  as element of trust, 36
  of government, 65–7, 70–1,
    161, 175–6
  reputation for, 31

confidence in government,
  declining, 62–6
  and changing issues, 66–7,
    70–1, 176–8
  contra early years of US, 96
  survey responses on, 59, 69
conflict of interest, 113
constitution, English, 148
constitution, US, 135
  ratification of, 147
constitutional treaty, EU, 150,
  154
constitutionalism, as two-stage
  choice, 138
contract, relational theory of,
  77
Convention, Annapolis, 141
Convention, Constitutional,
  141, 143–6
Convention, Philadelphia, 141,
  143–6
Cook, Karen, 152–3
cooperation
  experiments on trust and,
    43–58
  on the internet, 100
  network organization of, 120
  norm of, 87, 91
  trust as enabler of, 1, 35–6
  without trust, 53, 78–9
coordination of interests, 145
creative destruction, 94
crippled epistemology,
  122–3

Dean, Howard, 107, 116
Declaration of Independence,
  140
democracy
  audience, 174
  changing, 161
  participatory, 107, 116
  as threat to property, 164
  and trust, 95

Democracy Movement, in
China, 91–2
demographic changes, 5, 12,
36
deterrence
in a liberal state, 131
dilemma, social, 43
distrust
age of, 1–2, 4, 13, 35
asymmetry of trust and, 18,
23, 160
as cognitive, 27
competence and, 35–6
conflict of interest and,
17–18
and cynicism, 64
of elite government, 159
endemic, 32
and exclusionary groups,
129
expectations and, 33
experimental games and, 45
generalized, 11, 119, 127,
175
in government, 15, 39–40,
139–40, 160
in government in
contemporary US, 155
of government in EU, 150,
155
government failure and, 176
group vs. individual, 120
group-generalized, 119,
126–7, 133–4
of groups, 119
and hegemony, 159
intergroup, 15
on the internet, 114
and knowledge, 160
and lynching, 126–7
and paranoid cognition, 114
in peasant society, 10
and prisons, 93–4
as rational, 44–5

rising, and falling social
capital, 15
and rising trust, 13–14, 62
and separation of powers,
148
and terrorism, 118, 127
terrorism and ethnic, 10–12,
ch. 6
distrust, liberal
American, 149, 155
as collective wisdom, 156
contemporary, 179
in England, 149
in the EU, 150, 155
as foundation of liberalism,
39–40, 135
from Locke to Smith, 136–8
Montesquieu on, 149
and power dependence,
152–3
and US Bill of Rights, 140
DNA evidence, 131
Downs, Anthony, 170
Durkheim, Émile, 16, 69
dysphoric rumination, 113–14

East Europe, 154–6, 159
eBay, 99–100, 103
email, 103, 107, 111–14
pneumatique, 111–14, 117
risk of using, 117
embeddedness, 122
embourgeoisement, 129, 133
Emerson, Richard, 152–3
English Civil War, 137
epistemolgoy, crippled, 122–3
Estrich, Susan, 169
ethnic distrust, terrorism and,
10
euro, 150
European Union, 136, 150
and distrust in government,
155
as liberating, 151

evolution, theory of, 162
exchange as prisoner's
  dilemma, 20–1
expectations, 193
  and confidence, 29–31
  as conflated with trust, 33
  and generalized trust, 124–6
  and government, 167–8
  stable, 147–8, 159
  trust and, 27
experiments on trust, 43–58
  as a-theoretical, 71–2
  shortcomings of, 35–6, 51

familiarity and trust, 38–9
Federalist 10, 144, 155
Federalist 47, 148
Federalist Papers, 148, 154
Federalists, US, 146
Flexner Report, 163
fraud on eBay, 100
free trade, 141, 146
Fukuyama, Francis, 76, 81,
  95–6

Gamson, William, 69
Gates, Bill, 82, 166
General Social Survey, 60–2,
  72, 123
generational change, 12
globalization, 165
Goldwater, Barry, 162
Google, 99, 116
Gorbachev, Mikhail, 173
government, declining trust in,
  36
  see also under distrust
Great Society programs, 170
groups
  exclusionary, 14, 128–9
  extremist, 119, 122
  self–help, 115, 117

Hamilton, Alexander, 96, 142
Hayek, F. A., 178

Henry VIII, 140
Hewlett, William, 166
Hirschman, Albert, 12
Hitler, 143
Hobbes, Thomas, 22, 89, 133,
  137, 140
  two-stage theory of, 139
Hume, David, 142, 156
  on benefits of government,
    139
  and design of government,
    142, 167
  liberal distrust of
    government of, 39–40,
    137, 142, 159–60, 167
  and liberalism, 136–7, 157
  and Madison, 144
  risk aversion of, 137, 160
  on trust as from iterated
    interaction, 20, 37

incumbent re-election in US, 154
Indian federation, 146
Inland Revenue, 152
Internal Revenue Service (IRS),
  152–3
internet, the, *see* ch. 5
  as anomic society, 106
  anonymity of, 106
  and balkanization of science,
    116
  cooperation on, 100
  email on, 103, 107, 111–14,
    117
  and endgame effects, 105
  as fostering distrust, 114
  games on, 109, 117
  iterated interactions on, 99
  pneumatique, 111–14, 116
  political campaign on,
    107–8, 116
  and political participation,
    107
  power sellers on, 99, 102
  and privacy, 117

and reputation, 98
risks on, 113
romance on, 112
and science, 116
troubadours on, 112
internet capital, 117
Israel, 127
issues, changing, 164
  and distrust of government,
  161

Jacobs, Jane, 76
Japan, 71, 92, 157, 164–5,
  172, 177
Jefferson, Thomas, 142–3,
  145
Jim Crow laws, 126
Jobs, Steve, 82, 166
Johnson, Lyndon, 172

Kafka, Franz, 105, 111
Kant, Immanuel, 163
King, Anthony, 149, 155
Klaas, Polly, kidnap and
  murder victim, 169
Kohl, Helmut, 173–4
Krebs, Valdis, 108

laissez faire, 163, 165
law as relational, 88, 95–6
left–right economic dimension,
  161, 172
Leijonhufvud, Axel, 6, 8
liberalism
  against intrusions of the
  state, 135
  economic, 135–6, 145, 146
  political, 135–6, 148
libertarianism, social, 162–3
Locke, John, 7, 146, 157
  liberal distrust of, 136–7
  and liberalism, 160
  and trust of governors, 160
Lott, Senator Trent, 5, 193
lynching, 126–7

Madison, James, 135–48
  constitutional thought of,
  146
  and *Federalist* 10, 144, 155
  and *Federalist* 47, 148
  letter to Jefferson, 145
  liberal distrust of, 39–40
  158–60
  and liberalism, 144–6, 153,
  157, 178
  on Montesquieu, 144–5
  as politician, 154
  on popular sovereignty, 139
  as practical designer, 96,
  146–7
  on separation of powers,
  148
Magna Carta, 148
market for lemons, 102
marriage, 83, 105
Marx, Karl, 9–10, 94
McVeigh, Timothy, 4, 11
mercantilism, 138, 140–1, 163,
  177
militia groups in US, 119, 122
Mill, John Stuart, 163, 176
monetary policy, EU, 150
Monkey trial, 162, 172
Monnet, Jean, 151
Montesquieu, 138, 143, 145–6
  on separation of powers,
  148
  on small republics, 151
Montinola, Gabriela, 18, 193
motivation to be trustworthy
  as element of trust, 36
  in experimental games, 54
  of government officials, 70–1
  interest as, 16, 52
Mueller, John, 102, 115, 164
Murrah Federal Building, 4

Napoleon, 150
National Election Studies, 63
Nehru, Jawaharlal, 143

Neuman, Russell, 158
Neumann, John von, 85
NORC, 60
norms
  communal, 11, 37, 103, 115, 120
  of cooperation, 87
  of exclusion, 120, 121
  of reciprocity, 7, 54, 57

Oakeshott, Michael, 40
organizations
  social, 82, 83
  supposed trust of, 160
  voluntary political, 83

Packard, David, 166
Parent Teachers Association (PTA), 81
Parry, Geraint, 157, 159
Parsons, Talcott, 69
participation
  in groups, 83, 96
  political, 161
  social, and internet, 110
Pataki, Governor George, 170
Patterson, Orlando, 158
peasants, 10, 94
  absence of cooperation among, 9
  anomic society of, 10
  lack of class consciousness of, 9
pneumatique, internet, 111–14, 116
Poland, 29, 30, 159
power dependence and trust, 152–3
power sellers, 99, 102
prisoner's dilemma
  backwards induction in, 52
  iterated, 22, 45–6, 48, 52, 72, 86
  as model of exchange, 20–22

as model of trust relationships, 23
  motivations in, 45–6
  in test of cooperation, 43
  as test of encapsulated interest theory, 72
  and T-game, 48–9, 55
prisons, 93–4
proportional representation, in Germany, 171
Proposition 3 in 1998 in California, 168
Proust, Marcel, 4, 111
punishment
  and deterrence, 130
  and terrorism, 130
Putnam, Robert, 4, 12, 87, 110–11

Qaddafi, Muammar, 92, 143

racism in US, 126, 130, 155
Rahn, Wendy, 76
Rapoport, Anatol, 22
Reagan, Ronald, 155, 161, 173–4
referendums
  in California, 168–71
  on EU constitution, 154
reliance and trust, 23, 27, 74
reputation
  as absent in game experiments, 74
  in commercial dealings, 59, 101, 105
  and competence, 103
  as enabling cooperation, 22, 24–5
  as future oriented, 22, 102
  incentive effects of, 24
  as proxy for trustworhtiness, 120
  and trust as encapsulated interest, 19–20, 23–4, 39

Rhode Island, 143–4, 149
Riesenberg, Peter, 7
risk
  aversion, Hume's, 137, 160
  in experimental T-games,
    44–50
  on the internet, 101, 112,
    115, 117
  in trust relationships, 13, 19,
    22, 27–9, 37–8
Roosevelt, Teddy, 172
Rose, Richard, 69
Rotter, Julian, 32, 39, 42, 124

St Germain, 6, 8
Salem witch trials, 136
Schröder, Gerhard, 149, 166,
  174
Schultz, Theodore, 86
Schumpeter, Joseph, 94
science and the internet, 116
Scopes, John Thomas, 162,
  172
Seligman, Adam, 69
separation of powers, 148
September 11, 11, 30, 132,
  176
shunning, 10
slavery in US, 145
sleepers, terrorist, 129
Smith, Adam, 40, 136–7,
  139–41, 146
  on free trade, 141
  and liberal distrust, 138
  and liberalism, 157
  on mercantilism, 141
  Wealth of Nations, 140
social agenda, in US, 163, 166,
  171, 174–5, 177
social capital, 4
  blocking, 97
  in China, 92
  declining, 4, 66
  as including trust, 79

internet as form of, 106
  lack of valence of, 97
  Marx on, 94
  as means, 97
  as relational, 76
  as substitute for trust
    relationships, 79
  and television, 4–5, 12,
    110–11, 161
social intelligence, 57
Soviet federation, 146
Soviet Union, 3, 142, 156
  and Stalin, 142, 160
  trust in government of, 3
Spain, 11
spillover thesis, 157–8
Stalin, Joseph, 142, 160
Star Wars, 173
statism, 177–8
stereotyping, 11, 124–5, 130
  and discrimination in hiring,
    125
  distrust and, 128
surveys on trust, 58–71
  and conceptions of trust, 61
  and generalized trust, 124–6
  in US, 30, 35–6, 60
  weaknesses of, 36–7, 167
Sweden, 1, 36, 157
Sztompka, Piotr, 18, 24,
  29–30, 32–4, 156, 159

television and social capital,
  4–5, 12, 110–11, 161
terrorism, 10, 118
  and civil liberties, 118–19,
    129, 130–1, 133
  and ethnic distrust, 10; *see
    also* ch. 6
  and incentives, 133
  Islamic, 127–8, 133
  and liberal society, 134
  September 11, 11, 30, 32,
    132

T-game, 43, 46–9, 57
  with iteration, 48
  one-way, 47–9, 51–5, 57, 73
  with punishment, 49, 51
  and theories of trust, 56
Thatcher, Margaret, 40, 155,
    161, 173, 174
three-strikes law, 169–71
Thurmond, Strom, 193
Tierney, John, 155
Tocqueville, Alexis de, 66, 75
trust
  acting on, 18, 28–9, 33
  as behavioral, 33
  choosing to trust, 34
  as cognitive, 17, 27, 33, 38,
    56, 96
  cognitive limits on, 39
  conceptions of, 16–26,
    56–8, 61–2, 64, 74, 90,
    175
  cooperation without, 53,
    78–9
  declining, in government, 1,
    41, 67, 69, 157
  democracy and, 95
  dyadic relational, 40
  and email, 115
  as enabler of cooperation, 1,
    35–6
  as encapsulated-interest, 68
  and expectations, 124–6,
    147–8, 155–6, 159,
    167–8, 193
  expectations as conflated
    with, 33
  expectations as element of,
    27, 29–31, 33
  experiments on cooperation
    and, 43–58
  generalized, 69, 78, 123–6
  in government, 63–5, 67, 89,
    160, 176; as confidence,
    29, 65

  in government, impossibility
    of, 18, 41, 160, 167
  in government officials, 69
  and high stakes, 47, 55, 73
  immorality of, 27–8
  of institutions, 39
  interethnic, 37
  interpersonal, 14, 35–6, 58,
    60, 89, 124
  learning to, 125
  linguistics of, 2
  measurement of, 35–8
  misconceptions, 32
  from moral commitments,
    17, 32, 64, 68, 72
  as morally required, 57
  in networks, 8–9, 76, 103–4,
    116
  and ongoing relationships,
    19–20, 40, 90–1, 125
  and power differential, 34–5,
    113, 152–3
  prisoner's dilemma model of,
    20–3
  as proxy for trustworthiness,
    58–9, 91
  psychology of, 42
  as relational, 20, 51, 61–2,
    65, 117
  scale of, in government, 63
  spillover of, from one arena
    to another, 18, 157–8
  strong, 26
  theories of, 152
  as three-part relation, 19, 38,
    46, 73
  vernacular meanings of, 60,
    69
  weak, 26
  within government, 167
trust culture, 32
trust as encapsulated interest
  and communal norms, 120
  defined, 8, 17–23

experiments and, 53–4
and explanation, 26, 90–1
and group exclusion, 127–8
incentive structure of, 8
and the internet, 100, 104, 117
and interpersonal capital, 91
in networks, 8–9, 76, 103–05, 116
and power differences, 34–5, 152–3
and rational expectations, 31, 33
reputation and, 19–20, 23–5, 39, 71–2
risks in, 18–20
trust game, as mislabeled, *see* T-game
trust, mutual, 31, 44–5, 48–9, 55
trust scale
  NES, 63–4
  Rotter's, 42, 124
trustworthiness
  bases of, 56
  declining, 1, 2
  from character or disposition, 25
  from disposition, 26, 153
  as moral, 153
  from moral commitment, 25, 57
  norm of, 91
tryst, 2, 3
Turkle, Sherry, 109, 110, 112

Unabomber, 122, 128, 132
United Kingdom, 1, 11, 35, 36, 155
  and declining confidence, 62
  declining trust in, 157
United States
  and al-Qaeda, 175
  Amish in, 121

Articles of Confederation in, 136, 143
civil liberties in, 129
constitution of, 135, 138, 140–8
constitutional debates in, 154–5
and constrained government, 149
contemporary issues in, 172
de novo liberal government of, 148, 150
Dean internet campaign in, 107–8
and declining confidence, 1–2, 62
declining performance in, 89
declining social capital in, 4–5, 157
declining trust in, 1–2, 78
DNA evidence in, 131
environmental policy in, 171
extraconstitutional fourth branch in, 147
government failures in, 71
groups in, 66
Hobbesian foreign policy of, 133
institutional capital of, 88
interstate commerce in, 135
liberal distrust in, 149, 155
lynching in, 126–7
militia groups in, 119, 122
as new nation, 96
political parties in, 162
power of modern government of, 151
prisons in, 93
racism in, 126, 130, 155
referendums in, 168–71
September 11, 9–11, 127
social capital in, 66, 75

United States (*cont'd*)
  social libertarianism in, 163
  statism in, 177
  surveys in, 30, 35–6, 60
  Tocqueville on, 66, 75
  voter turnouts in, 63

value theory, cardinal, 85
Verba, Sidney, 158
Vietnam war, 155, 170
voters, ignorance of, 170

Wanamaker's department store,
  102
Washington, George, 144, 164
Wealth of Nations, 140
Williamson, Oliver, 95–6
Wisconsin v. Yoder et al., 121
women in US, 145
World Trade Center, 128,
  131–2

Yugoslavia, 126, 146

Made in the USA
Coppell, TX
15 March 2022

75009289R00118